LOW

NO SUGAR

How To Reduce Your Sugar Intake, Lose Weight & Feel Great

JESS LOMAS

JESS LOMAS is an author, editor and freelance film reviewer from Melbourne, Australia. She divides her time between covering classic and new release films for Quickflix, and writing about pop culture, health, diet and lifestyle for various publications.

WP

Published by:
Wilkinson Publishing Pty Ltd
ACN 006 042 173
Level 4, 2 Collins St Melbourne, Victoria, Australia 3000
Ph: +61 3 9654 5446
www.wilkinsonpublishing.com.au

International distribution by Pineapple Media Limited
(www.pineapple-media.com)   ISSN 2200-0151

National Library of Australia Cataloguing-in-Publication data:

Author: Lomas, Jess, author.

Title: Low sugar no sugar / Jess Lomas.

ISBN: 9781922178466 (paperback)

Subjects: Sugar-free diet.
                Sugar--Health aspects.
                Food--Sugar content.
                Sugar-free diet--Recipes.
                Weight loss.

Dewey Number 613.28332

Layout Design: Tango Media Pty Ltd

Cover Design: Tango Media Pty Ltd

Photos by agreement with iStock. Recipe photography by agreement with Jess Lomas.

The author wishes to thank Jeff Lomas for his assistance with photography equipment, and Wendy Katz for her food styling advice and equipment.

CONTENTS

Introduction 04

My story 06

Why sugar? 08

Is Low Sugar No Sugar for me? 13

Common questions 16

Your Low Sugar No Sugar action plan 22

    Do your research 23

    Commit.. 23

    The last hurrah!.. 24

    Cleanse the house 24

    Let's get started 25

    Week One: Begin to change your habits............ 26

    Week Two: Love yourself................................. 28

    Week Three: Eat to live.................................. 30

    Week Four: Check your progress 32

    Repeat 34

Cravings 36

Talk the talk while you walk the walk.................. 39

Travelling with a Low Sugar No Sugar mindset.................. 40

Supermarket tips 42

Recipes 47

Conclusion 126

Recommended reading.. 127

Index 128

INTRODUCTION

"Food deserves a constant and balanced presence in everyone's life. People will make good choices if given the information." — JAMIE OLIVER

"Quitting sugar" seems to be the diet du jour; its message of enjoying life with less added sugar is an express train reaching more people every day. Since the first edition of *Low Sugar No Sugar* was printed, media coverage and community interest in the low and no sugar movement has substantially increased. On a personal level, I have been overwhelmed by the feedback I have received about some of the *Low Sugar No Sugar* recipes and tips by reformed sugarholics, and continue to attract much interest and discussion when asked about my lifestyle changes.

The Low Sugar way of thinking is still considered somewhat controversial by health "experts" and by those with deep pockets and a vested interest in selling us their highly processed food-like products. Despite this, for every anti-quitting sugar news story, or statement by a health professional, there is someone whose life has radically changed through an altered lifestyle who is prepared to stand up and testify.

In 2003, the World Health Organization (WHO) released a report recommending that added sugar should account for no more than 10% of a person's caloric intake. In late 2013 the WHO was considering halving this amount to 5%, citing fears that excess added sugar in the diet could be contributing to heart disease, obesity, diabetes and tooth decay. Over the pond, the European Heart Network similarly released a report in 2011 recommending that sugar should account for no more than 10% of a person's daily caloric intake, but stated that 5% is a better objective.

The impact of the WHO's 2003 counsel was jeopardised by sugar industry lobbyists who threatened the US Government to withdraw their financial contributions to the WHO if the lowered recommendation was passed. Increasingly, studies and reports such as these send the sugar industry into panic mode, threatened that government policy may see them having to revise the levels of sugar used in their products at some point in the near future.

For those choosing to educate themselves today, however, there is no need to wait for government intervention. You are in control of reducing the amount of added sugar in your diet, not a corporation. You make this choice every time you eat a meal, visit a supermarket or dine at a restaurant. "This is going to require a tectonic shift in people's thinking," said Dr Robert Lustig in the article *Sugar: The Bitter Truth* from the January 9, 2014 edition of *The Times*. "But over time, such shifts are possible. It has happened at least twice in the past 30 years: one, smoking in public places; two, drunk driving. In each case, the science drove the policy, but public education softened the playing field."

At some point in your life you will have to pay for your health; the decision lies with you whether you pay for it now or later. Paying for it now means investing in yourself; investing time in education, money in whole foods and fresh ingredients, and making decisions that might set you apart from your family and friends. The alternative is to play Russian roulette with your health; you may be one of the fortunate few who get through life eating and drinking what they please and never really suffering the consequences, or you may sit with the majority and feel sluggish, lack concentration, have a weakened immunity, battle with weight gain, or at some stage face a diagnosis of diabetes, heart disease or worse.

There are countless diets and so-called healthy lifestyles out there battling for your attention and money, making promises that are hard to keep and setting out rules and restrictions that make it impossible for many to commit and see it through. Failure is imminent and almost a prerequisite that sustains the multi-billion dollar diet industry as stories are shared about weight lost and almost at once regained.

The No Sugar lifestyle is often "debunked" by nutritionists and relegated to the category of fad diets. As with any movement there are the extremists and there are those whose "rules" bend a little more flexibly. It's entirely up to you how far you take things. The message from the "experts" still seems to be, everything in moderation. This simplistic mantra has perhaps run its course; what is moderation when it comes to eating processed food and drinking sugary beverages? Is it once a month? Once a week? What happens if it's once or twice a day, as it is for many people around the world who find themselves addicted to the sweetness and emotional pleasure sugary food delivers, or for those who can't afford healthier options or worse yet, have restricted access to whole foods? Lowering the amount of added and processed sugars you eat *will* improve your wellbeing and in turn will help you appreciate the sweetness nature provides; anyone who tries to tell you differently is just trying to sell you something.

MY STORY

The declaration, "I've decided to stop eating so much sugar" is often met with two reactions: genuine interest in why, or scepticism that you've fallen for the latest fad. When I decided to change my lifestyle in April 2012, the no-sugar movement was beginning to pick up speed but was still a mystery to so many. I'm conscious to call it my lifestyle and not my diet because *Low Sugar No Sugar* is as much about enjoying life as it is about respecting your body. I had been advised many years before this that I needed to cut sugar out of my life, or at least reduce it, but it wasn't until this time that my brain finally clicked and I began to take the steps to change my life.

For some people, it is the hidden sugar that wreaks havoc in their life, foods they presume don't have high levels of sugar, such as store-bought sauces and dressings, pre-marinated meat, low-fat products, breakfast cereals, muesli bars and so on. I was already up to speed on reducing processed foods and increasing the amount of home cooked meals prepared from scratch; my sugar intake came from sources that I knew were loaded with the sweet stuff; chocolate, biscuits, cake, and the worst offender of all, soft drink. Yes I knew what I was feeding my body was bad but there

was one small problem standing in my way of cutting these foods out of my life; I was addicted to them.

Many will ridicule the idea of sugar as an addictive substance but the truth is the greater part of the Western population is currently living with a sugar addiction, the majority of which comes from soft drinks. Sugar feeds sugar, and so it wasn't surprising that one drink would never be enough to quench my thirst, and one row of chocolate didn't seem to fill that hungry gap in my stomach. Sugar became a part of my everyday life, a part that my brain told me I couldn't live without.

So how was all this sugar impacting on my life? Over the years my weight had yo-yoed from healthy to overweight; when I was younger I would bounce back more easily but in recent years I would find myself spending longer and longer at the gym, sweating it out and trying to lose the weight, all the while continuing to eat foods high in sugar. I found myself lethargic, even if I'd had eight hours sleep the night before; my immunity was almost non-existent, catching a cold if someone sneezed two rooms over from me, and struggling to get over it in under two weeks. I would have a "fuzzy" brain at work,

Low Sugar No Sugar is as much about enjoying life as it is about respecting your body.

struggling to maintain concentration and finding it nearly impossible to summon up enthusiasm for things, both work and social.

Despite knowing I needed to alter my attitude and diet, I continued with my old ways for several more years until a diagnosis of diabetes in the family made me finally stop and take stock of what I was doing to my body. I was sick of feeling overweight, being tired all the time, having a lowered immune system and not being happy with my reflection in the mirror, I finally decided it was time to make a change.

I gave myself a last hurrah, settling on Easter weekend for a feast to end all feasts, a sugar cocktail that made me instantaneously ill and gave me the final push to reduce the sugar in my diet. The following day I began, I went cold turkey and haven't looked back. Cutting sugar out entirely from day one is not for everyone, and my journey hasn't been without some hiccups, but from my experience I have learned several things about caring for ourselves that seem to have been

lost in an age where busy is glorified and convenience is worshipped.

Two years after taking on a Low Sugar No Sugar mindset there's no looking back. I lost ten kilos of weight and gained a new perspective on life, taking on each day with a renewed energy I hadn't experienced in years. I am constantly learning as I continue my Low Sugar No Sugar journey, always seeking to learn and understand more, and revising and creating new recipes that sustain this. Some of these recipes are included in this new edition, such as the delectable and incredibly easy cherry surprise chocolate cups and the gorgeous upside down chocolate pistachio cheesecake that adorns the cover.

Low Sugar No Sugar is as much your story as it is mine, whether you've been eating hidden sugars without knowing it or, like me, have had a sweet tooth for things you know aren't healthy, you have the power to change your life, to love your body and to live a sweeter life, with less sugar in it.

WHY SUGAR?

When we talk about sugar being addictive what we're really talking about is fructose. This is where some people get confused – fructose, as in fruit? Is there fructose in table sugar? What do I include and exclude? Suddenly something simple becomes more complicated.

When we eat fruit, the fructose comes wrapped in fibre, which slows the body's absorption of the sugar and minimises blood sugar spikes. Fruit also comes with the added benefit of multiple nutrients, vitamins and antioxidants, nature's helping hand. When we add fructose to other foods, what I'll refer to from now on as processed foods or excess sugar, the fibre is stripped and the amount of fructose is generally increased, putting unnecessary strain on our body, in particular our liver, to process it.

Fructose is a simple sugar that the body uses for energy, along with glucose. In small amounts, typically found in fruits and vegetables, the body can process fructose effectively, but once you add excessive amounts, through our convenience-food-dependent lifestyles and increased consumption of premade sauces, packaged foods, soft drinks, fruit juices and desserts, the body begins to struggle.

When you eat carbohydrates your body releases insulin to extract the glucose for fuel and cellular respiration. The liver only processes

Doing what is best for our bodies shouldn't be an overly complicated issue that needs a scientist to dissect the complex language for us.

approximately 20% of this thanks to an in-built mechanism that prohibits it from absorbing too much. Fructose, on the other hand, needs to be processed by the liver and is stored as a back-up energy source (glycogen). The problem arises when the energy-stores are full and you continue to consume fructose – what does the liver do? Working under increased stress, the liver begins to turn the excess fructose into by-products including triglycerides, which then undergo a further conversion into very low density lipoproteins (VLDL) and are stored in fat and muscle cells. What this means is that too much fructose equals an overworked liver and excess fatty acids and fat in the system, leading to a multitude of issues including (worst case scenario) diabetes, heart disease, insulin resistance and fatty liver disease. Most commonly the excess fructose manifests itself as weight gain, sluggishness and lowered immunity.

This is an extremely simplified explanation of why fructose is wreaking havoc on our bodies but for most people this is all they need.

On average the amount of fructose we now consume disrupts our body's natural appetite regulation, contributes to weight gain and overweight, suppresses our immune system by placing our vital organs under strain, promotes bodily inflammation, which can age your body and skin as well as promote illness and disease, and places strain on your pancreas, which can lead to insulin resistance and later

type 2 diabetes. Doing what is best for our bodies shouldn't be an overly complicated issue that needs a scientist to dissect the complex language for us.

What we must understand is what has happened to our food system and why the extra sugar that's being pumped into 80% of the items on sale in the average supermarket is making us fat and sick. When the science becomes overwhelming, take author Michael Pollan's advice, "We should not be eating anything our grandparent's grandparents wouldn't have eaten." Think about that the next time you go to your local supermarket and take in the aisles of heavily processed food.

A leading voice in the low-sugar movement is American paediatric endocrinologist

Sugar Cheat Sheet

GLUCOSE: Occurs naturally in plants and fruits, the human body can produce glucose when needed and it is used as energy by our body and converted into glycogen (muscle fuel).

FRUCTOSE: Occurs naturally in fruit, cane sugar and honey. The body can handle small amounts to use for energy but excess fructose is processed and stored by the liver where it is turned into fat if it cannot be used for energy. High Fructose Corn Syrup, more common in the United States than the rest of the world, is comprised of 55 per cent fructose and 45 per cent glucose.

SUCROSE: Commonly known as cane sugar or table sugar, it is comprised of 50 per cent glucose and 50 per cent fructose.

LACTOSE: The natural sugar found in dairy products, such as milk, is converted in the liver to glucose. Lactose is made up of one glucose monosaccharide bonded to one galactose monosaccharide.

MALTOSE: Also known as malt sugar, it is made of two glucose units bonded together and is the sugar found in beer.

Dr Robert H. Lustig. His YouTube lecture, *Sugar: The Bitter Truth* attracted international attention and by January 2014 had 4.2 million views (it is definitely worth your time to watch it online). Lustig argues that fructose is essentially a poison that has led to the rise in childhood and adult obesity, and that increased fructose consumption reduces satiety by blocking the release of leptin (an appetite-controlling hormone) and leads to overconsumption. He also believes that highly processed, sugary foods are contributing to metabolic syndrome, high blood pressure, excess abdomen fat, high blood sugar and insulin resistance, which can increase your risk of type 2 diabetes, stroke and heart disease, amongst other ailments.

Lustig's work follows on from John Yudkin's studies in the 1970s, and whose book *Pure, White and Deadly* has seen a recent revival in a new print edition. We will continue to see Yudkin's work referred to more in the media as the saturated fat debate (that it is the contested cause of heart disease) is re-examined under the microscope. Yudkin believed, as many are starting to see now, that excess sugar is the cause of many of our modern ailments and not saturated fat, as proposed

by Dr Ancel Keys, who decreed reducing saturated fat would lower cholesterol levels, and in turn heart disease rates. Of course, as you lower the saturated fat content of animal products you minimise the flavour of the overall food (fat tastes good), and so sugar is often pumped into a product to make the product palatable and saleable.

A quick trip to the dairy section of any supermarket, and a scan of the nutritional labels and ingredients list, will reveal the not-so-well-hidden secret of low fat dairy and low fat foods in general. Marketing and advertising executives are worth their weight in gold for selling us sugary foods wrapped in healthy jargon and appealing packages. Some of the words and phrases used to lure us in include "Premium", "No added sugar", "No fat", "Natural", "Gourmet", "Probiotic", "Organic", and "Field fruit" to convey fresh and healthy

ingredients. One "Lite 99% Fat Free" yoghurt had 13.5g of sugar per 100g; another with "Rich in calcium for strong bones" plastered across the front had 14.2g of sugar per 100g, with sugar listed as the third ingredient and "fructose" listed fifth. One blueberry yogurt had 19g of sugar per 100g and the average of five yoghurt brands I recorded had 15g of sugar per 100g. Hopefully this makes one thing clear to you, "low-fat" does not necessarily equal low sugar or a healthy choice.

As with any dietary advice or lifestyle choice there will be those on the other side of the fence telling you that studies aren't conclusive and there's no evidence to suggest fructose needs to be targeted as the enemy. The answer lies with you: what you feel like with less sugar in your diet, and how your body works on a processed food diet, only you can know what is best for you. Unfortunately it often takes a detox to determine this answer and most people place this idea in the too-hard basket.

Food manufacturers have been sneaking added sugar into their products for decades, at first stealthily until the public caught on. Now, despite the introduction of food nutrition labels, we've become so hooked on the products we love that many are addicted to the taste and can't help but keep buying the breakfast cereals, snacks, premade sauces and dressings that scream healthy on the label but in truth are far from it.

These days sugar is everywhere and in almost everything, forcing us to go back to basics and prepare meals from scratch. We've become experts at home prepared meals but we need to return to home *cooked* meals. Sticking to whole foods, good fats, fresh fruits and vegetables, a well-stocked spice rack, free range eggs and grass fed meats is our only hope to detox ourselves and future generations from the sugar addiction that holds so many of us hostage.

Taking your health into your own hands means getting back in the kitchen and re-educating yourself on how to prepare and cook real food, from simple breakfasts that start your day off with a bang to sweet treats that delight without throwing your liver in the deep end.

Sugar is an addiction that starts young and stays with us throughout life, whether we want to acknowledge it or not. What has taken so long to build cannot be changed in a matter of days or weeks. Changing to a Low Sugar No Sugar lifestyle takes time, patience and perseverance. The world is against you at every turn, tempting you to fall back on old ways, but the good news is that day by day more people are opening their eyes to the perils of excess sugar and the low sugar community multiplies its support network.

Sneaky Sugar

Even a stealth sugar watcher can be caught out at the grocery store. Look for ingredients that end in "ose" as these can indicate sugar is present; words such as glucose, sucrose, fructose, dextrose, galactose, lactose, levulose, maltose and glucose solids. Here are some other names often used on food packaging to indicate sugar as an ingredient:

Cane sugar
Cane juice
Evaporated cane juice
Dehydrated cane juice
Cane juice solids
Cane juice crystals
Agave nectar
Corn syrup
High fructose corn syrup
Crystalline fructose
Fruit sugar
Fruit juice concentrate
D-fructofuranose
D-arabino-hexulose
Malt syrup
Molasses
Barley malt
Caramel
Beet sugar
Brown sugar
Raw sugar
Honey
Golden syrup
Turbinado
Dextrin
Dextran
Maltodextrin

IS LOW SUGAR NO SUGAR FOR ME?

Let's clear one thing up right from the start. This is not a one-size-fits-all miracle cure, and this is not a diet, this is a lifestyle. Diets are designed to fail, to make us feel bad about ourselves, to make life difficult and to make someone else money. Making the decision to become more conscious of what you eat and reducing your sugar intake is a lifestyle change and a lifelong journey; it may sound corny but you must take each day as it comes, ride out the missteps and less than ideal choices, and congratulate yourself regularly for investing in your health and happiness.

I get asked a lot of different questions about my decision to rethink my sugar consumption. Most people ask me if I think they should change their sugar intake too; will it help with a particular problem or ailment. My answer is simple - we're all different.

The human body is an amazing machine but each machine was built a little differently to the next and each came with an instruction manual specifically written for us. The problem is that many of us can't read our manuals; they're written in a foreign language that we can't decipher. There are people who specialise in translating these manuals, and often charge large amounts of money to do so, but even they can never fully understand what the manual is saying. Only you can understand your body's manual, what works for you, what doesn't, how you feel eating this or abstaining from that, and what foods are the "right foods" by common standards but wreak havoc on your system.

Why can't we read our manuals?

There are several reasons why we can't decipher what our body is telling us. Firstly there's a general lack of education about food and how the body works. On a personal level, beyond covering the (hilariously out of whack) food pyramid in school I had very little teaching (or interest, to be honest) in nutrition until several years ago. Even now it is a learning process; day by day I add new information and rethink previous notions about my health. My opinion on the No Sugar movement has even changed since committing to it over twelve months ago, and you may find yourself in a similar situation as you go through the motions of reducing your sugar intake. The important thing to remember is that now it is *your* choice to educate yourself, it is *your* decision to allocate time, and sometimes money, to see what works best for your body, and the reality for many is that this isn't a priority. Furthermore, if you are an adult with children in your care, it is your responsibility to educate yourself in order to assist those who look to you for help, and those incapable of educating themselves.

Education is a gift to be shared with those around you and we're fortunate to live in an age where it is more accessible to more people than it has ever been before in history. We're not talking university courses and degrees here, although they have their place; what I'm referring to is the volume of books available to read and learn from, the lectures and more casual talks available through websites such as YouTube and Ted Talks (www.ted.com/talks), and the endless resources available on the Internet, most for little or no cost to the consumer. There are countless blogs to read and recipes being shared through sites like Facebook and Pinterest, and you too can be a part of this global act of sharing education and resources.

The second factor blocking our ability to read our body's manual is what we are putting in our mouths every day. Sugar feeds sugar, fat feeds fat and salt feeds salt. Your body becomes tuned to enjoy and crave what you feed it, and these three happen to be the most addictive things you could reach for. While this book isn't big enough to cover salt and fat in addition to sugar, the same principle applies, and it's the principle that big food manufacturers bank on. Make a product utterly irresistible and it's hard to pass that biscuit aisle without your brain

The Low Sugar No Sugar motto is simple: remove the everyday excesses and enjoy the occasional sweetness in life.

suggesting you pick up a couple of packets of your favourite chocolate dipped cookies.

When you take the sugar-goggles off you start to see the complex processes behind a simple packet of chips or can of soft drink; we're not simply being sold products but a way of life that becomes a part of our societal and cultural fabric. What would Christmas be without a steamed fruit pudding covered in custard, or Easter without the exchanging of chocolate eggs? Most of our holidays revolve around food, not a crime in itself except that the type of food being used as a celebration is no longer an occasional, seasonal occurrence, but a weekly staple in many homes.

The *Low Sugar No Sugar* motto is simple: remove the everyday excesses and enjoy the occasional sweetness in life. We're designed to enjoy sweet foods and an abundance of naturally sweet options have been provided for us by nature. Juicy berries, crisp apples, thirst-quenching slices of watermelon in the summer heat, these are not things to give up. Chocolate bars, cakes, fast food and pro-cessed, refined and packaged foods, these we can live without.

It may sound like an ostentatious claim but you cannot fail with a Low Sugar No Sugar mindset. Diets fail. Fads are soon replaced with the next "latest and greatest"; but a lifestyle change is a life-long journey. Of course there are going to be some setbacks, some bad days and sugar disasters of varying proportions, we are human and this is to be expected.

There are days when you'll reach for what's convenient instead of what feeds your body better, days you sleep in and find that toast with jam is all you can manage as you run out the door, and days when you overestimate what you can handle and eat one piece of chocolate too many. I've been there; believe me, it's okay.

What's not okay is feeling guilty about these moments, or berating yourself because you slipped up. Food should never be a source of guilt or pain. Take a moment to acknowledge your actions and think about how you can avoid making the same choice next time. Do you need to prepare a few more meals to have ready-to-go in the refrigerator for those days when the snooze button tempts you? How about removing the temptation before it's too late by not picking up a chocolate bar while doing the shopping this week? Make a mental note of what you can do differently, accept how you're feeling and then move on. Don't sit there stewing on what you've done or how you feel, and definitely don't wallow in self pity.

The most important thing to remember is not which fruits are lower in fructose or which brand of yoghurt is the healthiest, but that on this journey your number one goal each day is to love yourself. Through loving yourself and your body, making healthier decisions becomes easier. If you're ready to enjoy the sweetness life has to offer by eating less sugar, congratulations, it's a decision I know you won't regret.

COMMON QUESTIONS

How much fructose can I eat a day?

The American Heart Association advises the following guidelines for daily sugar consumption:

Men – 36 grams per day (9 teaspoons)
Women – 20 grams per day (5 teaspoons)
Children – 12 grams per day (3 teaspoons)

Currently the United States Department of Agriculture lists the average sugar consumption of adults as 22.2 teaspoons of sugar per day, while a teenager on average is said to consume a whopping 34 teaspoons a day. The World Health Organization recommends that sugar should make up no more than 5-10% of your daily calorie intake. It also counsels that this should be comprised of natural and not added sugars. When reading a nutritional label, look for no more than 6g of sugar per 100g or 100ml, as a general rule.

Can I eat fruit?

To eat fruit or not to eat fruit... that is the question. If fructose is the enemy then it goes without saying that fruit should be restricted or eliminated, right? Well, let's not be too hasty.

While the amount of fructose in fruit varies between berries, apples, citrus, melons etc, each have other benefits that suggest fruit in general shouldn't be thrown out automatically.

The human body can handle the amount of fructose in two pieces of fruit a day, which is, on average, what most people would consume. The issue arises when on top of the apple and banana you add a sugary drink like fruit juice, tea with sugar or a soft drink, a muffin with your morning cup of coffee, a tub of fruit flavoured yoghurt with lunch and a jar of pasta sauce on top of your spaghetti for dinner. You've not just stepped over the daily fructose limit but doubled or even tripled it.

Fruit should not be excluded from your diet unless you want to, in which case it's important you increase your vegetable consumption. Eating small amounts of seasonal fruit is not dangerous when added to a healthy, whole foods diet. Aim to include more berries, eat fruit whole with its skin, and avoid fruit juice, even home squeezed. Fruit juice ranks as high on the fructose scale as some soft drinks and is no substitute for a glass of water. Try adding berries or slices of fruit to your water for a boost of flavour and don't forget to eat the fruit after you've finished your drink. If making your own juice at home, stick to the 80-20 rule, 80% vegetables and 20% fruit, usually half an apple can suffice to provide enough sweetness.

Local and organic is best when it comes to fruit, and if both can't be achieved aim for at least one if your budget allows. When buying local fruit from a farmer's market or the farm door, you will find the apples smaller and generally not as sweet as their supermarket counterparts. You can also ensure the absence of pesticides and chemicals and be guaranteed that the product is fresh and hasn't been sitting in cold storage for months. Visiting a local market is also a good way to keep informed on what is in season and what types of fruit we should be eating at different times of the year.

If you want to follow the Low Sugar No Sugar action plan, fruit should be removed from your diet for at least the first thirty days, in order to allow your tastebuds to realign. At this time it's important to maintain and if possible increase your vegetable consumption.

Can I eat dried fruit?

Dried fruits are higher in fructose than whole fruit so are to be approached with caution. It's pretty hard to make a traditional Christmas pudding without dried fruit but it's easy to avoid snacking on it as a "healthy alternative". The healthier alternative is just to eat the whole fruit or snack on vegetable sticks, nuts or seeds.

As the fruit is dried it is dehydrated of the majority of its water content; this is great for preserving a food but in doing so the sugar content increases. Also, as the fruit is dehydrated its size decreases, meaning you can eat more without filling up as quickly, and you end up ingesting more than you would if you ate the whole fruit.

Be mindful of adding dried fruit to breakfast muesli, in trail mixes (unless you are actually going hiking and require the sugar hit) and in school lunch boxes for the kids. Save using dried fruit for those classic recipes that require it during the holidays.

Dates commonly pop up in many "healthy" recipes you'll find in cookbooks and online as a substitute to using white sugar. Dates are high in fructose and to be eaten with caution. As with any sugar substitute, they are okay to use sparingly as an alternative to refined sugar but should not become a common ingredient in your kitchen. You'll find your desire for sweet foods will decrease as you remove sugar from your diet and so using a small handful of dates in a dessert recipe now and then isn't going to hurt you. There are nutritional benefits to including moderate amounts of dates in your diet, including as a digestion aid, and they come packed with vitamins and minerals including magnesium and zinc. As always it's a personal decision.

What is the fructose content of some common fruits?

Lemon (1 medium) – 0.6 grams
Raspberries (1 cup) – 3 grams
Kiwifruit (1 medium) – 3.4 grams
Strawberries (1 cup) – 3.8 grams
Grapefruit (1/2 medium) – 4.3 grams

Orange (1 medium) – 6.1 grams
Banana (1 medium) – 7.1 grams
Apple (1 medium) – 9.5 grams
Raisins (1/4 cup) – 12.3 grams
Dried apricots (1 cup) – 16.4 grams
Dried figs (1 cup) – 23 grams

The Sugar Fix: The High Fructose Fallout that is Making You Fat and Sick, Richard Johnson and Timothy Cower, Gallery Books, 2009.

Can I eat honey and maple syrup?

If we're operating on fructose levels alone then honey and maple syrup should be on the "avoid" list. However, as with fruit, there's more to these two ingredients than just that.

Raw honey, a locally sourced product that hasn't been heat-treated, has an abundance of healing properties to consider beyond its fructose content. You won't find this type of honey on your supermarket shelf, anything sitting there has been heat treated and processed to remove all of the beneficial elements and leave only the sweetness. Your local farmer's market is a great source for raw

Swap tonic water with soda water or sparkling mineral water when mixing drinks. Tonic water is often mistakenly thought of as a sparkling water yet its sugar content ranks closer to lemonade.

honey, as is the Internet. It's amazing what you can source online these days; with many metropolitan areas boasting rooftop honey schemes ensuring local bees and minimal human interference. Raw honey ensures a premium product that has retained most or all of the beneficial enzymes, natural vitamins and antioxidants. It is anti viral, anti bacterial, promotes good digestive health and can be a powerful aid in treating allergies, particularly hay fever. A little bit goes a long way so you'll find a jar of raw honey will keep you going for many months, if not longer. If you can't source good quality raw honey don't substitute with a supermarket shelf brand, simply avoid it entirely.

As with honey, maple syrup comes in myriad of qualities and the more you pay, the purer the product will be. It is incredibly sweet so only a small amount goes a long way in recipes; we're not suggesting dousing a stack of pancakes in the stuff, as it is traditionally used for. Its health benefits include a high level of manganese, which is great for energy and in strengthening your immunity, and high levels of zinc, also good for the immune system and for reproductive health. Look for organic Grade A pure maple syrup and avoid maple "flavoured" syrup, which is a highly refined product lacking the benefits of the pure product.

Can I drink alcohol?

Yes … and no. While moderation is the key, not all alcohol is created equal when it comes to fructose levels. On the definitely-okay-to-drink list are red wine, beer, and straight spirits including gin, vodka and whisky; leave the mixer drinks such as Cola, fruit juice and tonic water out of your glass.

The level of fructose in winemaking grapes is considerably decreased by the time you drink the final product thanks to the

process of fermentation. While white wine undergoes this same process it still retains more sugar than red, with dessert wines and champagne joining it on the less than desirable but okay sometimes list. The sugar in beer is maltose, not fructose, and so is okay to drink, in moderation.

What are the safe sugar alternatives to use?

Dextrose, stevia and rice malt syrup are three easy sugar alternatives that you can usually find in your local supermarket. Each has both positive and negative aspects to its use. The recipe section of this book incorporates the use of all three sweeteners for variety's sake and can be interchanged as desired, although stevia is much sweeter and requires less to reach the same sweetness as dextrose and rice malt syrup. Some recipes also use fruit to sweeten.

Dextrose (glucose) is usually sold in bulk, is cheap, looks exactly like white sugar and is easy to substitute 1:1 in recipes calling for sugar. If not available at your local supermarket it can be found at health food stores or beer brewing supply stores. The negative of using dextrose is that it is still considered a refined sugar, produced commercially through the hydrolysis of starch. It is not a whole food and should not be treated as an "everyday" ingredient. You can also buy glucose syrup in most supermarkets in the baking supplies aisle; the recipes in this book use the granulated form of dextrose.

Stevia is a plant-derived sweetener gaining favour around the world. Even chocolatiers in Belgium have begun experimenting with stevia, offering a lower fructose option for those with a sweet tooth. The danger with stevia is that it is up to 300 times sweeter than white sugar so it's not as simple as a 1:1 substitute, as with dextrose. Also, depending on the brand and amount used, some stevia can leave a bitter aftertaste that may put some people off using it again. If used in the right quantities however, there should be no aftertaste. The other down-side to using stevia is the price; while it's more readily available on supermarket shelves, the price by weight is not relative to white sugar and may not be a viable alternative for those on a budget. Stevia is great to use in baking, home cooking, in coffee or tea and is also available in liquid form. The recipes in this book that use stevia are referring to the granulated product; if using liquid stevia you will need to convert the quantities.

Rice malt syrup is entirely fructose free and is low GI. It's made from fermented brown rice and cooked until it becomes a syrup. Rice malt syrup comprises 45% maltose, 3% glucose and the remaining 52% is soluble carbohydrates. Rice malt syrup is a complex carbohydrate with maltose (malt sugar) and a small amount of glucose. It can usually be found in the health food aisle of most supermarkets. It is relatively cheap and a little tends to go a long way but being a liquid is not as easy to substitute in recipes calling for granulated sugar and may take some experimenting to perfect. It's easy to use as a substitute for honey or maple syrup and is nice drizzled over yoghurt. After a year of developing recipes I find rice malt syrup is my preferred sugar substitute for cost, ease of use and taste but you may want to try all three for yourself and decide. It's important to check the ingredients label when buying rice malt syrup, any product that lists more than "organic rice" should be avoided.

What sugar alternatives are not safe to use?

Artificial sweeteners such as aspartame, often used in diet soft drinks, are manufactured, heavily processed and not recommended. Aspartame is often used in "low sugar" or "sugar free" products in the supermarket including cookies and desserts. While research into the effects of aspartame is ongoing, negative health effects are thought to include increased risk of cancer. Other fake sugars to avoid include sucralose, saccharine and alcohol-based sweeteners such as sorbitol. When choosing a sweetener, fructose is a consideration but it is far better to use a smaller amount of a whole foods sweetener such as raw honey than to use larger amounts of an artificial sweetener such as aspartame.

What foods should I restrict or eliminate?

It's dangerous to consign a food to a "banned" list, mostly because it will only serve to make you feel worse about yourself should you decide to eat it. The below are some processed foods worth avoiding (or checking the nutritional label) if you really want to give Low Sugar No Sugar a fair go. Of course there's nothing stopping you trying your hand at making a healthier, low sugar version of some of the below at home.

White bread
Raisin bread
Premade tortillas and wraps
Cakes, muffins and doughnuts
Cookies and crackers
Potato chips

Jams and breakfast spreads
Chutney
Salad dressing
Marinades and sauces
Asian sauces
Curry pastes and sauces
Dried fruit
Canned fruit
Preserved fruit
Fruit juice and fruit drinks
Soft drinks and cordial
Processed meats found in the deli department
Pre-marinated meat
Low fat foods including dairy
Flavoured milk
Baked beans and canned spaghetti
Breakfast cereals
Pasta sauce
Muesli and snack bars
Frozen pizza
Microwave dinners
Instant noodles with flavour sachets
Tomato sauce (approximately 25% sugar)
BBQ sauce (approximately 50% sugar)
Chewing gum
Lozenges

YOUR LOW SUGAR NO SUGAR ACTION PLAN

Now that you've decided to try and kick some sugar out of your diet what is your next step? Making the decision to prioritise your health is a great start but there are hard days ahead, I won't sugarcoat it, pun intended.

As you detox your body from its sugar dependence, some people may suffer from withdrawal symptoms, some may "relapse" before their detox is complete, and a lucky few will sail through relatively unscathed.

There are many schools of thought about how long the detox process takes, from the general 21 days to break a habit and 30 days to retrain your brain, to the more sugar-specific 8-week program run by Sarah Wilson's I Quit Sugar. It's different for every person, but what each number represents is a goal. Without a goal you will never realise when you've reached a milestone and so in lowering the amount of sugar you consume, whether you want to simply remove soft drinks and chocolate, or go the whole hog and cut sugar out entirely, I recommend the 30-30 rule.

The 30-30 rule is simple, and is in fact not a rule but a sign post to mark your progress. Aim for 30 days of mindful, low sugar eating and when day 30 draws to a close, look ahead to the following 30 days. Taking this journey one month at a time makes it more achievable than an open-ended time period that doesn't allow for special occasions or holidays. For some people 30 days will be long enough to change old habits and thinking, while others may have to look beyond one or two months until they feel in control of their cravings.

Of course there's a bit more to cutting out sugar than setting a 30-day goal, so keep reading.

1. Do your research

"So why have you given up sugar?" It's a question you'll be asked a lot once you let people know the decision you've made, and you might want to have an answer beyond "Fructose is bad!" Of course you don't need to justify your actions to anyone else, but you'll find most people are just generally interested, both in your health and in their own. You never know what difference your decision may have on someone close to you if you are able to succinctly tell them why you are doing what you're doing.

Take some time before D-day to read a variety of opinions on low-fructose or fructose-free living. There are a growing number of experts and lifestyle writers weighing in on it, some you may disagree with and some may

align perfectly with how you are feeling; the more you read, the easier it will be to decide where you fall on the Low Sugar No Sugar line: will you give it up entirely or just reduce processed foods and refined sugar in your diet?

When John Yudkin released his novel *Pure, White and Deadly* in 1972 he was a lone voice warning of the dangers of excess sugar in the diet. Skip forward to today where there is an abundance of easily accessible health information available to you, most of it for no charge.

Utilise the Internet and spend some time reading sugar-free blogs that offer testimonials of other people's journey quitting the white stuff; save any recipes that catch your eye to a folder for later use, cross-check facts and opinions, and make use of the online community, whether through blogs or Facebook groups, who are there to support each other.

2. Commit

Now that you know why you're kicking sugar to the curb, it's time to commit. It's easy to tell yourself, and even others, that you "need" to stop eating so much sugar (it's a similar conversation to "I need to exercise more" or "I need to stop watching so much television"), it's harder to actually follow through with it.

Once you know why you're changing your lifestyle, whether for health reasons, emotional reasons, as an experiment or even to support someone close to you on their sugar free journey, committing to the first 30 days becomes easier.

It's now time for you to share your commitment with someone close to you. You may choose to share it with one person, such as a partner, or many people, such as your entire social circle, it's entirely up to you.

Sharing your decision to change your lifestyle should not be a shameful prospect. To begin with, you are showing the other person how you value and trust their friendship by making them a witness to your journey, and in turn are asking for their help along the way. In essence, sharing your commitment makes you accountable and should help you stick to your new lifestyle by having someone to reach out to when times get tough. Through sharing with friends or family, questions may be raised that you hadn't yet thought of. How will you handle this temptation? What will you do if something unexpected happens? Now is a good time to get a second, third or fourth opinion before you dive in.

If you don't feel comfortable sharing your commitment with anyone just yet, commit to yourself and write yourself a letter. Explain why you are making this decision, how you felt before starting your Low Sugar No Sugar journey, and how you hope to feel after the first 30, 60 and 90 days. You might like to plan how you will tackle difficult situations like birthdays and holidays; will you embrace the spirit of the occasion and enjoy a piece of cake, or will you politely decline? Writing a letter is a great way to remind yourself down the track why you started this; you could even keep a journal as you go, to look back at how far you've come.

3. The Last Hurrah!

Some people may want to skip this step, in fact there's little sense and definitely no science to stuffing your face with as much sugar as possible but for some people, such as myself, this was the final nail in the coffin for ditching the white stuff.

Set a start date for your Low Sugar No Sugar journey, I chose the week after Easter and gave myself Easter Sunday to indulge in what, at the time, I had convinced myself I would miss. It was a sugar cocktail that made me feel ill almost instantly. It's the perfect activity for reminding you why you are about to take on an incredible detox, but if you're ready now, skip this step and move onto #4 - the cleanse.

Your last hurrah may take on other forms, from sitting down with your favourite block of chocolate, to going out to a special restaurant and sampling a couple of desserts, or it may be using a jar of sauce or dressing you know is chock-full of excess sugar, salt and other less desirables. Your last hurrah, like the rest of this journey, is unique to you. Set a date, indulge (or don't) and enjoy, then get ready for the next step.

4. Cleanse the house

Despite how it sounds, this step doesn't involve a traditional smoke ceremony, or getting in an expert to check the Feng Shui of your rooms. Cleansing your house begins and ends in your kitchen. Set aside a period of time where you can pull everything out of the cupboards and refrigerator. Read the nutritional labels and decide if it's a keeper or headed for the bin.

After the cupboards move on to the fridge and freezer. Remove any sauces, dressings, frozen desserts or ready-made meals disguising themselves as healthy alternatives to cooking for yourself. Those with a waste not want not mindset might like to donate the discarded items to a family member or friend who hasn't decided to join you on your adventure.

Now that you've cleared out the old it's important to introduce the new; head to your local supermarket or fresh food store and stock up on plenty of fresh vegetables, protein-rich meat, free-range eggs, good fats including avocados and full fat cheese, spices, nuts and seeds. When you begin your detox you'll notice changes in your body, and cravings, aches and pains will urge you to reach for something sweet; by stocking your fridge up with healthy options you're helping future you out of a sticky situation.

At this point it's best to remove fruit from your shopping list, it can be reintroduced after the first 30 days. It's important to abstain from anything overly sweet, even unrefined fructose in fruit, for at least the first 30 days as your body goes through detox and recovers. You'll be surprised when you take your first bite of an apple after detox at just how sweet it is, and in turn you might find you now need a smaller amount to satiate your appetite. Don't worry about missing out on the healthy benefits

of whole fruit; by increasing your vegetable intake, and diversifying the types of vegetables you eat, you'll have all your vitamin and mineral bases covered.

5. Let's get started

You've decided to lower or quit your sugar intake, you've read a few books or online articles, have an idea of how far you want to take it, have committed to doing it, either just to yourself or to a friend or loved one, have cleansed your kitchen of high sugar and highly processed foods ... now what?

At the back of this book is a collection of Low Sugar No Sugar recipes covering breakfast, lunch and dinner, as well as snacks, desserts and even recipes for children. Not all recipes will be suitable to make straight away, and some may not even take your fancy after you complete your first 30 low-sugar days (in fact, I don't recommend trying the dessert recipes until you're safely on the other side of Week Eight – the longer you can hold out the better). What the recipes do provide is a starting off point for you to begin experimenting. It is impossible to change to a Low Sugar No Sugar lifestyle without getting into the kitchen and cooking. This lifestyle relies on you getting back to basics, taking whole ingredients and creating healthy, wholesome meals from scratch. If you've never been confident in the kitchen, now is a great time to change that.

Remember to aim for the 30-30 rule, 30 days of mindful, low sugar eating before stopping to evaluate your progress, congratulate yourself on your achievements and look ahead to the coming 30 days. Break this down from week to week to make it easier.

Week One

BEGIN TO CHANGE YOUR HABITS

You've removed any high sugar products from your cupboards and have restocked your refrigerator with fresh, whole food ingredients, but once you leave your home you come face to face with a world of temptation. There's convenience stores to duck into for a quick sugar fix, someone's birthday at the office, an afternoon tea out with friends, or a work dinner that can't be avoided; these are scenarios you will continually face so it's time to work out your battle plan now.

The earlier you learn to say no to sugar, the easier the first 30 days, and your whole Low Sugar No Sugar (LSNS) experience will be. Week One is a great time to start substituting old sugar habits with new, healthier ones. Replace breakfast cereal with eggs served on steamed spinach, replace the lunchtime can of soft drink with a sparkling water, and take a platter of cheese into the office for a colleague's birthday in addition to the birthday cake, offering those without a sweet tooth an alternative. It's all about creative thinking to get out of old patterns and habits.

Avoid swapping to a lesser-of-the-two-evils option, even if it is only temporary. Swapping full strength soft drink for diet

soft drink is an unhealthy and unnecessary substitution. If soda is your Achilles' heel, try cutting back by 50% during the first week and drinking sparkling water in between, rather than switching over to the aspartame-sweetened beverages. If drinking coffee or tea is unbearable without a little sugar, try to reduce the amount you add. After Day 30 you can start experimenting with safer sugar alternatives such as stevia, although the ideal resolution is to enjoy your beverages au-naturel and sweetener free. For now, reduce the added sugar to your drinks by half and aim for zero added sweetener by the start of Week Two.

Drinking tea to help ease into the detox period is a cheap and easy way to reduce cravings, aid digestion and calm the nerves as you kick your sugar habit. Boasting high levels of antioxidants, the below teas can cleanse your system, boost your metabolism and help flush the liver of toxins. Try burdock root tea, cayenne pepper tea, dandelion tea, fenugreek tea, green tea, milk thistle tea or turmeric tea.

By the end of Week One you may not have experienced any substantial withdrawal symptoms beyond the odd craving or two. This will of course depend on how much sugar you used to eat, and in what forms, highly processed and "obvious" sugars (such as in soft drink and desserts) or "hidden" sugars in pre-packaged products, dried fruit or fruit juice.

If you've already experienced cravings, the best way to banish them is to eat a protein rich snack or meal and drink a glass of water, or try some of the cravings buster tips from page 37. Often a Week One craving is emotional or mental rather than an actual physical craving, which will come later in Week Two. You're so used to eating or drinking something that the break in habit causes you to think about eating or drinking that thing more frequently than usual. By actively eating something that will fill you up, you squash the craving in its tracks before your brain can try and convince you to give in.

Week One Tips

1. Substitute old sugary habits with new LSNS ones.

2. Replace soft drink and fruit juice with sparkling or plain water.

3. Cut down or go cold turkey, it's up to you. Either reduce the frequency of sugary foods, aiming to get down to zero servings by the start of Week Two, or eliminate sugar entirely from day one.

4. If you're experiencing cravings, eat a protein rich snack or drink a glass of water.

Week Two

LOVE YOURSELF

The first two weeks of sugar detox will be the hardest as your body nudges you at every opportunity to eat something sweet. Week Two is the time to stick to your guns and ride the detox wave. Symptoms you may experience include headaches, body aches and sweats, interrupted sleep, nausea and overwhelming cravings. You may experience none, some or all of these.

It's important during Week One and Two to make time to relax. Try not to do any extreme exercise but stick to low impact activities such as yoga, walking or gentle swimming. Your body will be going through a large change and it's likely you won't be feeling at your peak during this time, so there's no need to add extra stress by attempting to start rock climbing now or entering yourself in a marathon. Equally, this is not a time to sit and do nothing, waiting for the cravings to overwhelm you. Going for a moderate walk is a great way to stave off any cravings as well as clear your head.

Chromium and magnesium supplements are great to take during Week One and Week Two of your Low Sugar No Sugar action plan. Chromium helps regulate blood sugar levels and can help ease sugar cravings, while magnesium helps stabilise mood and can help you cope better with the stress of a detox.

If possible during Week Two, make an appointment for a massage or facial, some activity where you can be pampered and where the toxins leaving your system can have a helping hand. If a massage doesn't fit into your budget, try asking a kind-hearted partner, friend or family member for one to help you on your way. Having a sauna or sitting in a steam room is also great for both relaxation and toxin release, as long as you make sure to rehydrate during and afterwards.

Loving yourself can also mean going to see a movie, taking time to finish reading a book

that's been sitting there for months, going on a date night, booking a weekend away somewhere, anything that will remind you of the pleasures in life that don't rely on sugar, and anything that nurtures your soul. Physically, Week Two will be the hardest so it's important to remember to love yourself and be kind to yourself during this time.

Again, utilise the cravings buster tips on page 37. Your prime goal this week is to take it easy and nourish your body through the detox. Work may be unavoidable, but keep your weeknights free of social activity unless absolutely necessary. Your energy levels may be low, and physically you may start to feel like you're coming down with a cold. Putting unnecessary stress on your system by still trying to do it all and see everyone will only make Week Two more miserable for you.

By now you should have zero added sugar in your diet; soft drinks and fruit juices should be replaced with sparkling or plain water, coffee and tea should be without sugar or not drunk at all if you can't handle it straight. You should be focusing on increasing your vegetable intake; if you were always a "meat and three-veg" type of person, now is the time to up the quota, why not make it five different vegetables? Aim to eat something green with every meal and remember protein and good fats are your helping hand to staying full and staying away from sugar.

Week Two Tips

1. Your diet should now include no added sugar; it's time to face the detox head on.

2. Above all remember to love yourself, this is a special week to nurture your body through the withdrawal symptoms.

3. If possible book in a massage or facial, or have a sauna or foot spa to help eliminate toxins and ease the withdrawal process.

4. Chromium and magnesium are great supplements to take at this time.

Week Three

EAT TO LIVE

How are you feeling? Hopefully by the beginning of Week Three you're starting to feel more like yourself again, or perhaps starting to feel like a new person. By now the withdrawal symptoms should be subsiding, but don't be surprised if they linger a little longer, be gentle on yourself and take time out of every day to relax.

As Week Three begins you can start getting a little more active, perhaps booking in a game of tennis with friends or increasing the length of your workouts. You should start to feel a renewed energy with all the whole foods you've been eating and sugar you've been avoiding. Your body may have gone through a period of shock as it waited day in day out for the usual fructose fix, but by now it's caught on to your new lifestyle and the foggy, listless you of two weeks ago should be a distant memory. Don't worry if this doesn't quite sound like how you're feeling, it's different for everyone and it may take you a bit more time to start feeling better. Stick to the cravings busters and low-impact exercise, and re-evaluate at the end of the week.

Week Three is all about eating to live. When you reduce the amount of excess fructose in your diet, you release the body's natural ability to regulate its appetite. You may have asked yourself why it is you fill up so easily eating a big steak or even cheese and crackers compared to a packet of cookies that may disappear in one sitting without you even realising. Sugar doesn't satiate your appetite. Simply put, you don't fill up because the body's three appetite hormones, insulin, leptin and cholecystokinin don't respond when a flood of fructose comes in, and so you keep eating more and more. Once you reduce your fructose intake, as you should have done by now, you'll find yourself more aware of when you are truly hungry as well as finding you feel full from eating less food.

Avoid balsamic vinegar and stick to extra virgin olive oil or apple cider vinegar on your salad. True balsamic vinegar is aged for years, water is removed and the sugar becomes more concentrated. Despite this, true balsamic vinegar in moderation is okay as it boasts various health benefits including boosting immunity thanks to a polyphenol antioxidant. The problem is that most balsamic vinegars available in the supermarket are mass produced and are considered condiments rather than pure vinegars. It's likely that the balsamic vinegar in your cupboard hasn't gone through the lengthy fermentation process that is traditionally used in Italy. Supermarket balsamic vinegar is often cheaper as the product contains caramel colouring to make it darker and sweeter.

Congratulations on making it this far and regulating your appetite by reducing the fructose in your diet. Now that you're not filling up on empty calories, you're truly eating to live, cutting out the rubbish to make way for whole foods that nourish your entire body. By forcing yourself to prepare meals from scratch it's likely you've gone for simpler meals that require fewer ingredients and don't take long to cook. The good news is now that you're realigning your taste buds to appreciate the abundant flavours in all foods, and not just sweet foods, a simple meal delivers the same satisfaction as a more elaborate recipe.

Focus on food in Week Three. Start a recipe folder and begin adding recipes you might like to try after your first 30 days of low fructose eating. Spend a little extra time at the super-market, greengrocer or farmer's market this week getting to know some vegetables you may not have tried before. Speak to the shop assistant and ask questions about how to store and prepare the vegetable, you'll be surprised at the knowledge they'll have to impart. The same applies for your local butcher or fish-monger, if you haven't spoken to them before, now is the time to strike up a relationship, ask about cuts of meat or specials.

Enjoy the abundance of delicious foods nature has to offer, make the time to cook and learn about new ingredients, and soon the flavour and the experience will more than com-pensate for the ease of buying mass produced, packaged food.

Week Three Tips

1. Increase activity this week if you feel up to it.

2. Start a recipe folder of low fructose recipes to try after the first 30 days are over.

3. Focus on food – speak to your local greengrocer about their produce.

4. Try a new vegetable this week.

Week Four

CHECK YOUR PROGRESS

You can see the finish line on the horizon, you're almost there! Thirty days seemed like a long time when you began your Low Sugar No Sugar journey but you're about to reach the end, so it's time to check your progress and reflect on how you went, congratulate yourself on this incredible achievement, and look ahead to the next 30 days.

Take some time this week to sit down and think or write about how you found the first 30 days. If you've been keeping a journal about your journey this will help you remember those first two rocky weeks when cravings were high and withdrawal symptoms were hard to ignore.

Focus on one particular bad experience and one positive; it may have been a time you gave in to a craving or you may have thought negatively about yourself and your progress. Think about the bad experience first and how you might avoid repeating it in your upcoming 30 days. Was it a temptation that you know can be avoided next time? Can you now detect the warning signs that might lead to you thinking negatively about your progress? Was it a particular person that helped stir up these

feelings? Can you talk to them about it? Make a resolution about how to deal with the issue if it arises again.

Now let go of the negative and move on to the positive experience, hopefully there will be more than one you can call upon at this time. Why was this moment great? Did you navigate a week of birthday parties without touching a slice of cake? Did you manage to wean yourself off your soda addiction? Did you wake up one day feeling happy within yourself? Whatever it was that stood out to you about the last 30 days, take some time to enjoy it all over again. These are the moments that will provide fuel for you to keep going into the next 30 days of Low Sugar No Sugar, and beyond. These are the moments you can call upon when your next craving hits or when you begin to doubt your motivation or progress.

This last week is for reflecting on what worked and didn't work for you, your strengths and weaknesses, and how you can know and understand them better to help you over the next 30 days. Being honest with yourself at this point is crucial.

At the end of Week Four you can reintroduce fruit into your diet if you feel like it. It's good to start with berries and work your way on from there, perhaps try adding them to your breakfast to begin with. If you've stuck with LSNS over the first 30 days, and removed fruit by the end of Week One at the latest, you might be surprised by how sweet it tastes now. Be careful not to fall back into old habits and let fruit be your "gateway drug" to sweeter things; stick to one piece of fruit a day for the next 30 days before returning to two pieces of fruit a day after that (Week Eight).

Week Four Tips

1. Sit down and evaluate your first 30 days of LSNS, what worked and didn't work.

2. Choose one negative and one positive experience to learn from and to call upon to get you through the next 30 days.

3. Slowly begin to reintroduce fruit by the end of the week, stick to one piece of fruit for the next 30 days before returning to two if desired.

4. Congratulate yourself for an incredible achievement – 30 days into your new Low Sugar No Sugar lifestyle!

5. Look ahead to the next 30 days.

6. Repeat

Once you've reflected on the past 30 days, taken time to revel in your success and celebrated your achievements, it's time to look forward to the next 30 days. Low Sugar No Sugar works best when broken down into achievable time periods. Thirty days is only one month to change your life, and as one month draws to a close it's time to get ready for the next.

You may still be struggling with your sweet tooth, with saying no to sugar or dealing with the lingering detox symptoms, be assured that the next 30 days will be easier, there's no looking back!

The good news as you enter your second block of 30 days is that you won't have to deal with any more withdrawal symptoms, the detox is done! As long as you stick to the LSNS motto you won't have to ever repeat those two weeks. Keep up the home cooked meals using fresh whole food ingredients, avoid processed food, utilise supplements to suppress cravings, eat a green vegetable with every meal, do some form of exercise or movement every day, and keep educating yourself. When looking for tips to get through the second block of 30 days, look to Week Three and Week Four for guidance; you've done the hard yards and thrown sugar to the curb, now it's about being vigilant and not reintroducing it.

At the end of the second block of 30 days (Week Eight) it's time to increase your fruit to two pieces a day, if you decide. You may find that you're happy with your one serving or you might be eager to reintroduce more. It's also time to start considering sugar alternatives, such as dextrose, rice malt syrup or stevia.

If you're ready, and if you want to, you can start looking at the sweeter recipes at the back of this book, perhaps starting with one of the snack ideas before moving onto a larger dessert. As with any of the information in this book, this step is not a rule, merely a suggestion. There is no need to consume any of the sweeter treats in the recipe section; they are there only for those times when you want something sweet but not overly-processed. I am not recommending you make a sweet treat a daily or weekly occurrence, or even force yourself to try a recipe at this stage.

Depending on your commitment level to Low Sugar No Sugar, whether you are cutting back on sugar or cutting it out, remember the 30-30 rule. Take your journey 30 days at a time: reduce or eliminate, stop and evaluate, congratulate and look forward to the next 30 days. Focus on feeding your body whole foods instead of processed foods, invest in your education by allocating time to reading books and articles or watching documentaries about food, get back in the kitchen and cook from scratch, love yourself through the positive moments and even more through the weaker times, and above all don't forget to enjoy life with the occasional treat if you choose to.

LSNS Action Plan checklist

☐ I have read at least 1 book or 3 articles about the low-fructose or fructose-free lifestyle

☐ I have decided how far I want to take my LSNS sugar – cut back or cut out entirely

☐ I have committed to myself, my family or friends for at least the first 30 days of LSNS

☐ I have set a date to begin LSNS and had my last hurrah

☐ I have cleansed my house of sugary and processed foods

☐ I have stocked my refrigerator and pantry with fresh whole foods

☐ Week One – I have changed my habits and switched sugar for LSNS alternatives

☐ Week Two – I have cut added sugar down to zero and removed fruit from my diet until the end of Day 30

☐ I have taken time to relax, had a massage or did something I enjoyed

☐ I reduced my exercise to low impact

☐ I tried a cravings buster

☐ Week Three – I increased my vegetable intake, focused on whole foods and tried a new vegetable

☐ I increased exercise if I felt up to it

☐ I started a recipe folder for low-fructose ideas

☐ Week Four – I evaluated the negative and positive experiences of my first 30 days

☐ I reintroduced 1 piece of fruit a day at the end of the week

☐ I congratulated myself for making it through 30 days

☐ I have planned for the next 30 days

CRAVINGS

It's not a question of if but when your body will start trying to convince you to feed it sugar. Depending on your individual lifestyle, and whether your sugar intake came mostly "hidden" in foods or in the form of chocolate, sweets or soft drinks, you'll find the detox stage will vary. Some may make it through with hardly any cravings while others may feel incredibly sick.

The first two weeks will be the hardest, especially if you're a daily snack eater. I remember getting to the end of the first week, having batted off several cravings, and thinking, "Where are all those detox symptoms I'd heard so much about? This is going to be so much easier than I thought!" Of course as

I entered the following week my body decided to let me know just how much pain it could put me through. As I said before, you may experience some of these symptoms or none, each body is different.

- Headaches
- Body aches and pains
- Fever
- Irritability
- Interrupted sleep
- Nausea
- Cold-like symptoms
- Overwhelming cravings

10 sugar-busting tips for cravings

1. Eat more protein and fat. When that little voice in your head starts suggesting a slice of cake, squash it with a high-protein meal with a side of healthy fat such as avocado or a piece of full fat cheese like haloumi.

2. Get a helping hand from chromium. Taking chromium supplements helps regulate blood sugar levels and can help ease sugar cravings, which commonly occur when your blood sugar crashes. The recommended daily dose is 600-1,000mg a day, taken with food.

3. Take a magnesium supplement with your chromium. If you only add two supplements to your Low Sugar No Sugar routine make it these two powerhouses, especially during your first 30 days. Magnesium is similar to chromium in that it helps regulate blood sugar and eases sugar cravings but magnesium's greatest power is in stabilising mood and emotions, in turn helping you cope better with the stress of going through a major detox.

4. Zinc is another great supplement to take while weaning off sugar. One of the side effects of zinc deficiency is decreased taste bud sensitivity, meaning you're more likely to reach for the high sugar, salt and fat foods to feel satiated. By taking a zinc supplement during your first 30 days you may find it helps amplify the taste of all food, hopefully deterring you from reaching for something sugary.

5. Snack on a sweeter vegetable such as a carrot until your sugar craving subsides.

6. Have half a glass of full cream milk or a serving of full cream cheese, not only will the fat satiate your appetite but you'll begin to notice the natural sweetness of the lactose once you remove added sugars from the diet.

7. Try yoga. According to yoga guru Tara Stiles, the best pose for a sugar craving is a seated meditation with arms in a "V" as it allows your mind to refocus. Maintain this pose for 3 minutes.

8. Distract yourself by doing an activity such as going for a walk or vacuuming the house. Physical activity is better than sitting down to watch television, as it's likely your cravings will continue during the advertisements when you're bombarded with food ads.

9. Don't replace sugar with artificial sweeteners hoping to curb your cravings, research has not shown this to be the case and you're simply replacing one bad habit with another and possibly promoting your cravings even more.

10. Brush your teeth. It may seem like a strange way to curb a sugar craving but it serves two purposes, sending a message to your brain that you have finished eating, and also distracting you from your cravings.

Late night cravings

For many people the most dangerous time of the day are the hours after dinner but before bed, when a late night craving rears its ugly head and your thirst for sugar kicks into high gear. Before you try out the snack recipes at the back of the book, you might like to ask yourself why your cravings are particularly bad at this time of the day, and what changes you can implement to alter this behaviour.

Is it boredom? Habit? Is one activity feeding another? Can you sit down and watch television without wanting something to munch on? Can you have a cup of tea without reaching for a biscuit or a slice of something sweet?

Try these late night cravings busters:

Drink water. Dehydration is one of the biggest causes of food cravings. It sounds simple but if you fill up on water there won't be room for anything else.

Clean up after dinner. As soon as you've finished dinner clean the dishes and pack any leftovers away in the refrigerator. Removing food from sight and having a clean kitchen are small reminders that eating time is over and there should be no picking at the remnants from dinner when you walk into the kitchen, which inevitably can lead to searching for something sweeter.

Move away from the television. Sometimes we find ourselves sitting in front of the TV watching whatever garbage is on; it's been a long day and we just want some mindless entertainment. Mindless eating goes hand in hand with mindless entertainment.

Switch the television off a couple of nights a week and play a family board game or read something that requires concentration or delivers pleasure. If you can do an activity with someone else, concentrate on something other than your cravings and gain pleasure from something other than food then you're more likely not to reach for, let alone think about, a sweet treat after dinner.

Have a shower or a bath. This may seem like an unusual tactic but it can work. A warm shower or bath late at night can signal to your body that you're getting ready for sleep, helping you relax and unwind from a long day. Most of us don't get enough sleep during the week so apart from helping you overcome your cravings you'll also be one step closer to reaching your eight hours a night.

Remove the source. This requires foresight and the ability (also called willpower) to put down the packet of biscuits at the supermarket. By making your home a no-fly zone for packaged biscuits, chips, ice cream and chocolate bars you're one step closer to kicking late night snacking to the curb.

TALK THE TALK WHILE YOU WALK THE WALK

Positive language concerning food and eating habits is vital to sticking to a healthy lifestyle, which means negativity is strictly forbidden. Even if you feel positive in mind and spirit, all it takes is one friend having a bad day, or one overly opinionated family member or co-worker to derail you. While the common diet, designed to fail, counts on you breaking the rules and feeling shame, embarrassment and even self loathing, when changing your lifestyle and lowering your sugar intake it's these "failures" that will make you stronger in the long run. It's the moments you slip, overindulge or make the less desirable choice that will cement for you how your body works on low sugar and how it feels when you fall back on old habits.

Talking your health and your choices down is a great way to fast track self-loathing and won't make achieving your health goals any easier. Remember, what you used to eat is in the past and cannot be changed, what you might eat in the future is not worth your time worrying about, but what you feed your body at this exact moment is completely in your control. Above all, **you are not what you eat**, you are a complex and beautiful person and each day offers another opportunity to learn and grow.

Don't let these phrases come out of your mouth:
- I can't eat that.
- I'm not allowed to eat that.
- I wish I could eat that.
- You're so lucky you get to eat that.
- I'd kill for some chocolate.
- I just ate some chocolate, I feel terrible.
- I've failed.
- I cheated.
- I couldn't even last a week, I'm pathetic.
- I should be doing better by now.

Replace negative talk with affirmations:
- I choose to eat this.
- I choose not to eat that.
- I hit a bump in the road but tomorrow is a new day.
- I am more than what I eat.
- I'm doing so well.
- Today I am happy, healthy and in control of my life.
- What can I learn from this?

TRAVELLING WITH A LOW SUGAR NO SUGAR MINDSET

Even if you're not watching the amount of sugar in your diet, the prospect of an airplane meal is hardly met with enthusiasm by most passengers. Preparing for a low sugar trip involves just that, preparation. Whether travelling by road, sea or air, there are many things you can do and pack that will help you avoid settling for the sugar-laden snacks on offer in road stops and airports.

Travelling by car is the easiest way to maintain a low sugar diet, as you can pack whatever you like and use an esky or cooler bag to keep the items fresh. Road trips are perfect for premade sandwiches and salads, soup in a thermos, leftover roast meat and vegetables; it's easy to adapt most healthy meals for the road.

Equally, domestic flights can be easy to prepare for with sandwiches and salads, just keep your fellow travellers in mind and don't pack anything too pungent or messy.

International air travel becomes more complicated when you factor in liquid restrictions, and coming home from an overseas holiday may be difficult to prepare for out of a hotel room, but you can certainly pack a meal and a few snacks when leaving your home port.

On a recent flight, a breakfast tray was placed in front of me containing a cheesy omelette with mushrooms, sausage and hash brown, fruit bowl, muesli bar, croissant with butter and strawberry jam, orange juice and strawberry flavoured yoghurt. As has become habit, I read the nutritional label on each item.

The small muesli bar had as much sugar as a small chocolate bar, with dried fruit and added sugar it packed 16g of sugar per 100g. The orange juice should have been labelled an orange flavoured drink, its ingredients read; orange juice concentrate, sucrose, citric acid, permitted food conditioner, flavouring and colouring (wow, sounds healthy). If one simply ate the omelette and the fruit bowl it would constitute a reasonably healthy meal, as far as airline food goes. However, add in the drink, yoghurt and muesli bar, plus the jam if you spread it on your croissant, and you've just ingested a sugar cocktail at 40,000 feet.

The breakfast shines in comparison to the snack pack offered on a lot of carriers, containing biscuits, chocolate covered nuts and muesli bars. It's easy food, served to the masses quickly and efficiently. Of course you can't expect anything better when flying, unless you're lucky enough to fly business or first class, even then the food is designed to be easily reheated in the air, and is ultimately cost effective and uniform, offering each passenger the exact same eating experience. Fresh food is rarely uniform, even if it appears to be; there are always small differences. There's no getting around eating airplane food, except that is, not eating it at all.

Try planning ahead and packing zip lock bags full of carrot sticks, celery and cucumber wedges. Pack a salad in a disposable container, a small bag of nuts and seeds, or make a batch of vegetable frittatas in small muffin liners and wrap in cling film.

Once you get to your destination, seek out your closest supermarket or organic grocer and stock up on healthy snacks; this is where a mini fridge in your hotel room comes in handy. Depending on where you are travelling and your budget, consider renting an apartment through websites such as Airbnb.com, or a boutique hotel with kitchen facilities to break up the need for eating out.

Before leaving on your holiday, while taking the time to research which landmarks to visit and hotels to stay in, spend some time online researching the food culture in your intended destination. A simple Google search of "Where to eat healthy in...", "Health food stores in..." or "Organic shops in..." will bring up articles as well as blog posts giving you a multitude of options to choose from. Bloggers have become an integral part of trip planning, getting out in their home towns and doing the hard work for you, providing tips and recommendations to you for free, often highlighting cuisines and areas of town left out of guide books.

There are times in a trip where you have less power to control what you are eating, including the return flight home. Learn to choose your battles and not to stress too much over what you may have to eat over a day or two in transit. If you find yourself falling off the wagon while on holidays, just remember that when you get home you can start Low Sugar No Sugar again, and that it's all a learning experience for next time.

Remember to ask yourself, how can I learn from this experience? And of course, if you're visiting somewhere like Belgium with its famous chocolate culture, or France with its famous desserts, it's perfectly fine to treat yourself without remorse; life is to be lived after all!

SUPERMARKET TIPS

Once you understand the layout of the supermarket - how the products, aisles and shelves are specifically designed to sell, sell, sell, then avoiding the excess sugar becomes a lot easier. Of course the best prevention is to avoid packaged foods entirely but sometimes the best laid plans go awry and a box of something less than desirable ends up in the shopping trolley.

1. Stick to the perimeters of the store. Here you'll find the freshest food, from produce to meat and dairy. Of course this rule can bend somewhat, you'll have to venture down the aisles for spices, oil, toilet paper etc.

They say two-thirds of your dinner plate should be plant based, and the same applies to your shopping trolley. If your local supermarket lacks variety or quality when it comes to fruits and vegetables, seek out your nearest speciality produce store and stock up!

2. Read labels. Okay, another no-brainer but for many a trip to the supermarket is quick-in and quick-out, grab the essentials, be tempted by a special, and zip through the self checkout. Slow down. Take the time to read the label. What are the ingredients? Do you understand what they all are? Can you even pronounce them? How much sugar and salt is in the product? Is there a better option?

Serving sizes can be deceiving so it's always best to base your decision on the 'Per 100g' column. When buying dairy, look for sugar content under 6g per 100g. Ingredients must be listed in descending weight order so if sugar appears first, drop the packet immediately and run.

3. Dedicate time for food shopping. This is really an extension on #2. If you're in a rush, you're more likely to grab what's close or on special. Set aside an hour one week to go to the supermarket alone or with your shopping partner and walk the aisles reading and comparing labels. Pick up the brands and items you would usually buy and read the packet, compare it with competing brands and see if another product is a better choice.

Once you've dedicated a shopping trip to this it will reduce the overall time of subsequent trips as you'll know which products to add to your trolley and which aisles to skip completely.

4. Plan ahead. Write a shopping list and stick to it! Put your invisible blinkers on and know where you have to go; avoid wandering the aisles and letting yourself be tempted by things you don't need. If it helps, plan the coming week's meals and snacks on the weekend and write your list according to what you'll need. Be firm. Do not deviate from the list and no matter how tempting something looks, be strong.

5. Don't shop hungry. It's an age-old rule that makes a lot of sense. If you go to the store on an empty stomach you'll likely come home with bags full of stuff you really shouldn't be eating. Biscuits, ice cream, chips, convenience meals, they all look tempting when our stomach starts to grumble. Worst case scenario; buy a small bag of nuts when you begin your shopping to nibble on as you make your way through the supermarket.

6. Resist the impulse buy and avoid front of store and end of aisle displays. The people who manage supermarkets think they're pretty clever, I should know I used to work in the industry. Huge displays now adorn the entryways to most supermarkets and the ends of aisles, advertising the latest competition or presenting a towering display of a super special that's such a great deal you'd be crazy not to put two of each flavour into your trolley immediately. Their goal is obvious, catch you unawares and make you seize on the impulse buy.

Occasionally the produce department specials will seep into this area, and you might be lucky to snag yourself a fresh bargain or a close-to-use-by-date special, but more often than not we're talking slabs of soft drink and towers of boxed biscuits and chips. Stick to your plan, stick to your list, and resist the impulse buy!

Ingredients must be listed in descending weight order so if sugar appears first, drop the packet immediately and run.

7. Avoid anything labelled Fat Free. Fat isn't a bad thing, our brains actually need it to thrive and it satiates our hunger, but the real reason to avoid foods labelled Fat Free is that when fat is taken out of a food, sugar or other substitutes (including milk powder or salt) are usually put in. The product still has to taste good enough to sell (and eat), right? Go full fat dairy for butter, milk, yogurt and cheese. Not convinced? Rule #2 – read and compare the labels!

8. Avoid products with more than 5 ingredients. There are many reasons why we reach for a bottle of premade sauce, a sachet of flavouring to add to a casserole, or an entire meal frozen in a cardboard box. Laziness and lack of preparation rank highly on the list; as we move further away from home cooked meals to home prepared meals.

No one is suggesting you need to grow your own tomatoes, harvest and process them into your own tomato sauce and paste, but a basic pasta sauce has less than 5 ingredients;

it's a good rule of thumb to keep in mind when perusing the supermarket shelves.

9. Bring the kids along. Controversial, I know. Many will suggest leaving the kids at home when doing the food shopping to avoid the "inevitable" temper tantrum in the cereal or biscuit aisle, and sometimes this is the best plan of attack. For the other times, treat your children with the intelligence they have and deserve, and discuss what you're buying, and not buying, with them. If you begin educating them about food choices and the power of advertising from a young age, you may be surprised how well it sticks.

10. Treat yourself. Don't forget that a treat now and then goes a long way. Becoming more aware of the hidden excess sugar in products you used to consume daily or weekly, and removing them from your shopping trolley opens up room for that occasional block of dark chocolate or even a Low Sugar No Sugar dessert from the recipes section of this book.

SHOPPING LIST STAPLES

"Let food be thy medicine and medicine be thy food." HIPPOCRATES, 431 B.C.

Stock your supermarket trolley up with the following spices and products to help you on your Low Sugar No Sugar journey.

Cinnamon: Regulates blood sugar levels, helps prevent insulin spikes after meals and controls cravings. Cinnamon is also a great source of manganese, iron and calcium.

Cloves: Helps regulate blood sugar levels and along with coriander, nutmeg, cardamom and cinnamon, can naturally sweeten your food and reduce cravings.

Turmeric: Supports insulin production and regulates blood sugar levels. It's also great for helping with inflammation, which can occur during the detox period.

Cacao: Raw cacao is a must-have in your Low Sugar No Sugar kitchen. Made by cold-pressing the bean, it's loaded with magnesium, which can help regulate mood, reduce stress and cravings; it also raises serotonin levels and doesn't contribute to insulin spikes. In addition to being a powerful antioxidant, raw cacao is most helpful in curbing chocolate cravings and addiction with its rich and deep taste. Find good quality raw cacao in specialty supermarkets or health food stores and add to smoothies and desserts for a chocolate hit. Don't confuse cocoa for raw cacao. Cocoa, found in supermarkets in the baking aisle or powdered drinks section, is a refined version of raw cacao, roasted at high temperatures resulting in a lower nutrient level.

Coconut oil: Aids in digestion, provides energy, helps control blood sugar levels and insulin secretion. An incredibly versatile food product, coconut oil is stable at high cooking temperatures, can be substituted in any recipe for other types of oil, and a teaspoon is a quick and easy snack to ward off a sugar craving. Look for organic virgin coconut oil in your supermarket, specialty grocer, health food store or online.

RECIPES

Dips and Sauces

When entertaining or just wanting a snack, buying a dip or bottle of sauce from the supermarket is one of the easiest ways to ingest unnecessary sugar. There are safer options when it comes to store-bought dips, such as hummus or tzatziki, just be sure to always check the nutritional label and ingredients list.

Watch out for "skinny" dips, which, like low-fat products, will usually have a higher sugar content. On a quick trip to the dip aisle I found a "skinny" tzatziki with 6.3g of sugar per 100g, a "skinny" sweet potato dip with 9.2g of sugar per 100g, and a sweet chilli and lime dip with 9.3g of sugar per 100g.

The real danger lurks not in the dip section but in the sauce aisle. Between tomato sauce, BBQ sauce and salad dressings there is an alarming amount of hidden sugar that's not so well hidden. A survey of the nutritional label will show you that on average Thousand Island dressing has 22.3g of sugar per 100g (20.3g in the 99% fat-free version), Coleslaw dressing has 16.9g per 100g (26.2g in the 99% fat-free version), Whole Egg Mayonnaise has 2.2g per 100g but 13g per 100g when you go for the 65% less fat version, and 21g per 100g when you choose the 99% fat free version. Sugar is often the second or third ingredient listed, which also gives you a good indication of the sweetness of the product.

Take a look at a bottle of tomato or BBQ sauce and you'll see on average there's 29g of sugar per 100g in tomato and 54g per 100g in BBQ sauce. Choose a steak sauce and you're looking at 34.8g, while sweet chilli sauce can have a whopping 42.2g of sugar per 100g.

When you discover how easy it is to make your own homemade condiments and dips you may never go back to buying store bought. There might be times for the sake of convenience you are forced to buy one but you'll automatically notice the unnecessary sweetness.

Having a food processor or stick blender at home becomes a necessity when making food from scratch and needn't break the bank as there are many economy models on the market. Dips and sauces can be made and stored in the refrigerator for several days but are best made as needed; an added bonus is this ensures minimal waste.

SALSA VERDE

1 cup flat leaf parsley

³/₄ cup extra virgin olive oil

1 tsp ground fennel

1 tsp ground coriander

2 small cloves of garlic

½ cup of lemon juice

1 tsp lemon zest

1. Add parsley to the bowl of a food processor and pulse until broken down.

2. Add olive oil, spices and lemon juice and zest. Pulse until combined.

CHIMICHURRI SAUCE

This sauce is perfect paired with red meat, as a marinade or drizzled over vegetables or salad, it's so fresh and versatile.

2 cups flat leaf parsley, no stems

½ cup coriander

4 garlic cloves

½ cup extra virgin olive oil

2 tbsp white wine vinegar

Salt and pepper to taste

Add all ingredients to the bowl of a food processor and blend until combined. Add more olive oil if the mixture is too dry.

CREAMY SPINACH DIP WITH PARMESAN STRAWS

Creamy spinach dip

1 cup Greek yoghurt

2 cups baby spinach

$1/4$ cup fresh coriander (cilantro)

2 tbsp extra virgin olive oil

$1/4$ cup chopped pine nuts (optional)

$1/4$ tsp ground nutmeg

$1/2$ tsp ground coriander

Salt and pepper to taste

1. In a food processor combine yoghurt, baby spinach and fresh coriander. Set aside.

2. In a pan heat oil and add chopped pine nuts. Toast until brown then add nutmeg, coriander, salt and pepper and stir through the nuts. If not using nuts simply add spices to the yoghurt mixture.

3. Combine yoghurt mixture and nut mixture, taste and add seasoning if needed.

4. Store in the refrigerator.

Parmesan straws

1 sheet puff pastry (store bought is fine)

1 egg

1 tbsp water

$1/3$ cup shredded parmesan cheese

1 tbsp dried oregano

1 tbsp dried basil

Salt and pepper to taste

1. Pre-heat the oven to 190°C/375°F.

2. Defrost puff pastry and line an oven tray with baking paper.

3. Beat the egg and water together and brush mixture over the pastry surface.

4. Sprinkle parmesan cheese, oregano, basil, salt and pepper evenly over the pastry and press down either using your hands or lightly rolling over with a rolling pin.

5. Cut pastry into strips depending on desired thickness.

6. Twist each strip by holding the top and bottom and gently rotating, careful not to break the pastry.

7. Lay each strip on the baking tray and cook in the oven for 10 - 15 minutes until brown and crispy, turning the straws over halfway through the cooking time.

8. Remove from the oven and allow to cool before serving.

ROASTED CAPSICUM
BUTTER BEAN DIP

½ cup pine nuts

1 cup roasted capsicum

½ cup cooked butter beans
(or other white bean)

1 tsp salt

1 tsp ground cumin

Pinch of black pepper

1. In a small pan over a low heat, dry toast the pine nuts.

2. Add roasted capsicum, pine nuts, butter beans and seasoning to the bowl of a food processer and pulse until combined. You can keep the dip chunky or process until more pureed.

* Roast the capsicum yourself by removing the capsicum core and laying the flesh on a baking tray, drizzling olive or coconut oil over the top and seasoning with salt, pepper and garlic cloves. Roast in a 190°C/356°F oven for 25 minutes or more if needed. You can also use pre-roasted capsicum; just check the sugar and salt levels on the nutritional panel.

LOW SUGAR TOMATO SAUCE

1 cup crushed tomatoes

1 tbsp apple cider vinegar

½ tsp sea salt

½ tsp smoked paprika

1. Using a stick blender or food processor, pulse the crushed tomatoes until they form a puree. You can skip this step by using a good quality, low salt and low sugar tomato paste or passata, though you'll likely want to omit any extra salt if using this option.

2. Add apple cider vinegar, salt and paprika and pulse to combine. Taste and add additional seasoning if needed.

BBQ SAUCE

170g tomato paste

1 tbsp rice malt syrup

3 tbsp apple cider vinegar

1 tsp chilli powder (optional)

1 tsp paprika

1 tbsp Worsterchire sauce

½ tsp salt

Whisk all ingredients together and store in the refrigerator for up to 2 weeks.

Make as needed rather than in bulk.

THOUSAND ISLAND DRESSING

½ cup Greek yoghurt

1 tbsp white vinegar

1 tsp rice malt syrup (or liquid sweetener of your choice)

1 tbsp tomato puree

1 tbsp finely diced onion

1 tbsp finely diced dill pickle

½ tsp paprika

Salt and pepper to taste

1. Whisk yoghurt, vinegar, rice malt syrup and tomato puree together.

2. Stir in diced onion, dill pickle, paprika, salt and pepper.

3. Store in the refrigerator for up to 2 weeks, make as needed rather than in bulk.

MAYONNAISE

2 free range egg yolks

1 tsp mustard powder

1 tbsp white wine vinegar

1 cup extra virgin olive oil

Salt and pepper

1. Combine egg yolks, mustard powder, white wine vinegar, salt and pepper in a food processor and blend until combined, slowly adding the olive oil through the feed tube.

2. To make aioli add 1 garlic clove to the mixture when processing.

Breakfast

Sugary breakfast cereals, jams and spreads be gone! Breakfast is the easiest meal of the day to get right once you start thinking outside the box.

After sugar rations were abolished following the end of the Second World War, breakfast cereal producers started adding more and more of the white gold to their recipes and consumers couldn't get enough.

It wasn't until the 1970s that sugar levels in breakfast foods were questioned but even today breakfast foods demand their own supermarket aisle and most people think cereal and toast for weekdays, and bacon and eggs on the weekend are their only options. Breakfast foods are big business and big money and we've all fallen for their marketing tricks.

Even breakfast cereals promoted as healthier options can have an alarming level of sugar in them. A popular bran cereal has 13.6g of sugar per 100g, trying to sell itself on a panel boasting one serving of this provides 44% of your daily fibre needs. Children's cereals are even worse as they don't attempt to conceal their sugary nature, boasting chocolate flavouring (and 36.5g of sugar per 100g!), dried fruit in place of whole fruit, cartoon characters, and free toys, cards or rewards schemes. Sure, they'll start your day off with a bang but you'll quickly fizzle as your sugar high becomes a sugar crash.

There are no rules to what you can eat to kick-start your day. Asian diets include fish; one traditional Egyptian breakfast dish includes chickpeas, green vegetables, a hard-boiled egg, garlic and tahini, and a Turkish breakfast plate can include cheese, olives, eggs and cured meats. Increasingly the Western idea of breakfast is being adopted across the world, including sugar-laden, highly processed cereals, white toast with jam or chocolate spreads, deep-fried foods, pancakes and waffles, and stodgy food-like products that do little to fuel your body for a busy day.

Get creative with breakfast; any type of food can be eaten at any time of the day, all you need to do is retrain your brain to stop thinking that the only foods you can eat for breakfast are what we've been sold as "breakfast foods".

BRUNCH SALAD

3 cups kale, stems removed

3 tomatoes

1 lemon

4 free range eggs

200g pancetta (or bacon), thinly sliced

1 avocado

½ cup lemon dill sauce

1. Pre-heat the oven to 180°C/356°F. Thickly slice the tomatoes and lemon into rounds and lay on a lined baking tray. Spray with olive or coconut oil and season with salt and pepper. Bake in the oven for 20 minutes or until roasted. Remove and let cool.

2. Remove stems from kale, cut kale leaves into chunks and transfer to a small bowl. Pour over half the lemon dill sauce (page 87) and using your hands massage the sauce into the kale leaves until tender, approximately 2 minutes.

3. Place eggs in a small saucepan and cover with cold water. Bring to a boil and cook eggs to liking; 2 minutes for a soft boiled egg, 4 – 5 minutes for medium boiled (depending on the size of the eggs). Alternatively you can poach the eggs. Once boiled egg has cooled, peel the shell off.

4. In a small fry pan cook the pancetta for 3 – 4 minutes until crisp, drain on paper towel.

5. Slice the avocado to desired thickness.

6. Assemble the salad starting with the kale, adding the avocado, eggs, roasted tomato, pancetta and finishing with the remaining lemon dill sauce and roasted lemon. Season with salt and pepper if needed.

GRILLED MUSHROOMS
WITH ITALIAN BAKED BEANS

2 cups dried beans
(or substitute with canned
beans and skip step 3) *any
type of beans you want to use

5 tomatoes

1 brown onion

½ cup finely diced celery

3 cups beef (or vegetable)
stock

1 cup water

1 tbsp Worcestershire sauce

2 sprigs fresh oregano

2 sprigs fresh rosemary

2 medium flat mushrooms
(such as Portobello)

Salt and pepper to taste

1. Rinse dried or canned beans and set aside.

2. Dice tomatoes, onion and celery and add to a heavy based pan. Sauté in a drizzle of olive oil then add the beans, stock and water.

3. On the stovetop cook beans on low for 2 – 3 hours, testing for tenderness after 2 hours.

4. Add the Worcestershire sauce, oregano and rosemary after 1 hour.

5. If using canned beans, add beans to tomato, onion and celery followed by ½ cup of beef stock, herbs, salt and pepper. Warm through for 15 – 20 minutes.

6. Add a drizzle of olive oil to a frying pan, remove stems from the mushrooms and cook for 2 minutes each side until tender. Serve each mushroom with a spoon of beans and slice of roasted tomato (optional) on top.

There are limited options when it comes to store-bought baked beans as a small number of brands dominate the market. Read the nutritional label and you might discover a tin of baked beans has on average 13.8g of sugar per 100g, as well as a high level of salt.

LEMON GINGER GRANOLA WITH ROASTED STRAWBERRIES

1 cup rolled oats

¼ cup shredded coconut

2 tbsp coconut oil

1 tbsp rice malt syrup

Zest of 1 lemon

1 tbsp lemon juice

1 tsp ground nutmeg

1 tsp ground ginger

250g strawberries

1 tbsp lemon zest

1. Preheat oven to 180°C/356°F and line a baking tray with baking paper.

2. Slice strawberries in thirds and spread on the tray. Roast for approximately 20 minutes. Replace the baking paper on the tray and prepare the granola.

2. Combine rolled oats, shredded coconut, coconut oil, rice malt syrup, lemon zest and juice, ground nutmeg and ginger in a bowl.

3. Spread mixture evenly over lined tray and bake in the oven for 10 – 15 minutes or until golden brown, careful not to let it burn.

4. Remove from oven, let cool and store in an airtight container.

5. Serve with milk or natural yoghurt, topped with roasted strawberries and a sprinkling of lemon zest.

SWEET POTATO PANCAKES

2 medium sweet potatoes

1 small onion

2 free range eggs

½ cup rice flour (or plain flour, plus more as needed)

2 tsp salt

1 tsp pepper

Coconut oil for cooking

Sour cream and smoked salmon for serving

1. Peel the sweet potatoes and grate using a box cutter or food processor.

2. Finely dice the onion and add to the potato mixture.

3. Beat the eggs and stir through the potato and onion followed by the flour, salt and pepper. Add more flour if the mixture is too wet and doesn't hold together in your hand.

4. Add enough coconut oil to a frying pan to shallow fry the pancakes, approximately ½ cup, you may need to add more as you go.

5. Take spoonfuls of the mixture and drop into the pan, pressing down gently with the back of the spoon. Cook for a few minutes on one side before flipping and cooking for a further two minutes, they should be golden brown in colour and crispy.

6. Serve plain or with sour cream and smoked salmon.

TOMATO & BACON BREAKFAST SOUP

1kg tomatoes

1 fennel bulb

2 tbsp olive oil

2 tsp sea salt

1/2 tsp black pepper

1 1/2 tsp smoked paprika

6 rashers middle bacon

2 cups chicken stock

1. Preheat oven to 160°C/320°F. Halve tomatoes and thickly slice the fennel and spread out on an oven tray lined with baking paper. Drizzle with olive oil and sprinkle with salt, pepper and smoked paprika. Roast until tender, approximately 1 hour.

2. Dice bacon and cook in a pan. Reserve half for garnish.

3. Using a blender or a stick mixer puree roasted tomatoes, fennel, chicken stock and half the bacon.

4. Serve with remaining diced bacon sprinkled on top.

SPINACH AND ZUCCHINI FRITTERS WITH SPICED RICOTTA

1 zucchini

2 cups baby spinach leaves

1 egg

1/2 cup milk

2 tbsp flour

Zest of 1 lemon

Salt and pepper to taste

1 cup ricotta

1 tsp cinnamon

1 tsp cardamom

1 tsp ginger

1. Grate the zucchini and place in a clean dishtowel or piece of muslin cloth. Secure the end and squeeze the excess water out.

2. Steam the baby spinach and drain any excess liquid in a clean dishtowel or piece of muslin cloth.

3. Combine zucchini in a bowl with baby spinach, egg, milk, flour, lemon zest and salt and pepper.

4. Heat a small amount of olive or coconut oil in a pan and drop spoonfuls of the batter in.

5. Cook each fritter for about 4-5 minutes each side, cut open a test fritter to ensure it is cooked through.

6. In a bowl mix ricotta with cinnamon, cardamom and ginger.

7. Serve warm fritters with a dollop of spiced ricotta on top.

MEDITERRANEAN BREAKFAST PLATE

Delicious breakfast ideas don't come easier than this. Taking inspiration from the Mediterranean, where longevity and happiness are directly attributed to lifestyle and diet, this breakfast plate can be eaten at any time of the day.

(SERVES 1)

2 eggs

Pinch of sea salt

1/2 tsp ground cumin

1/2 cup hummus

1 small Lebanese cucumber, diced

1/2 tomato, diced

1/4 cup black olives

1 cup shredded lettuce, any variety

25g Greek feta cheese, crumbled (optional)

1. Whisk the eggs with sea salt and cumin.

2. Heat a small fry pan and scramble the eggs, set aside.

3. Use a good quality store-bought hummus or prepare your own by adding 200g of cooked chickpeas to the bowl of a food processor with 1 tbsp hulled tahini, the juice of half a lemon, 50ml extra virgin olive oil and salt and pepper to taste. Mix until smooth in texture.

4. Place all components on a place and drizzle a small amount of extra virgin olive oil over the top.

STRAWBERRY CHIA PUDDING

2 cups full fat milk (or any nut milk)

1 cup fresh or frozen strawberries

1/2 cup shredded coconut

1 tbsp rice malt syrup

1 tsp cinnamon

1/4 cup chia seeds

1. In a blender or using a stick blender puree strawberries, milk, shredded coconut and rice malt syrup.

2. Transfer mixture to a bowl and whisk in chia seeds and cinnamon.

3. Leave for one hour, whisking the mixture every 20 minutes.

4. Serve at room temperature or chilled, topped with extra coconut and strawberries if desired. Store in the refrigerator.

PECAN OAT BREAKFAST BARS

1 cup chopped pecans

²/₃ cup brewed coffee (or water)

2 cups rolled oats

2 tbsp linseeds

2 tbsp chia seeds

¹/₃ cup coconut oil

¹/₂ cup almond butter

2 tbsp rice malt syrup

2 tsp cinnamon

1 tsp nutmeg

1. Soak chopped pecans in the brewed coffee (or water) for 1 hour.

2. Preheat the oven to 180°C/356°F. Strain the pecans from the remaining coffee or water and spread over an oven tray lined with baking paper.

3. Roast the pecans in the oven for 10 minutes then set aside to cool.

4. In a bowl mix rolled oats, linseeds, chia seeds, cinnamon and nutmeg.

5. In a small saucepan melt coconut oil, almond butter and rice malt syrup together. Remove from heat and set aside.

6. Add pecans to the rolled oat mixture followed by the coconut and almond butter mixture.

7. Pour mixture into a lined baking tin and press down using the back of a spoon or your hands.

8. Refrigerate mixture for 1 hour or until set then cut into bars and store in an airtight container in the refrigerator.

* You can replace rice malt syrup with raw honey, simply omit the syrup from step #5 and add raw honey during step #6.

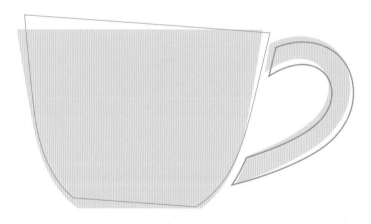

SWEET POTATO & BACON MINI LOAVES

Navigating a low sugar breakfast can be difficult when you first start, especially when you want a slice of bread in the morning but you don't want to lather it in jam and other condiments. Try this savoury sweet potato and bacon loaf that's delicious hot or cold, and gives you a head start on hitting your daily vegetable quota. Serve with a smear of butter or try ricotta or smashed avocado.

(SERVES 2)

½ cup white flour

½ cup wholemeal spelt flour

½ tsp baking soda

¼ tsp baking powder

1 tsp cinnamon

2 eggs

½ cup coconut oil

¼ cup rice malt syrup

1 medium sweet potato

1 small zucchini

1 tsp sea salt

1 tsp black pepper

2 rashers short bacon

1. Preheat oven to 180°C/350°F.

2. Sift flours, baking soda, baking powder and cinnamon into a bowl, set aside.

3. Whisk eggs, coconut oil and rice malt syrup together and fold through the dry mixture.

4. Grate the sweet potato and zucchini, season with salt and pepper and add to the mixture.

5. Divide the batter between two mini loaf pans. Alternatively, use one large loaf pan and increase the cooking time.

6. Dice bacon and sprinkle evenly over the top of each loaf.

7. Bake in the oven for 50 – 60 minutes. Test it is cooked through when an inserted skewer comes out clean.

POACHED EGGS ON AVOCADO AND WHITE BEAN MASH

Poaching eggs can be a daunting prospect for many home cooks but like everything, practice makes perfect!

(SERVES 1, MULTIPLY AS NEEDED)

2 free range eggs (at room temperature)

2 tsp white vinegar

1/2 avocado

1/2 can of cannellini beans

1/4 cup lemon juice (fresh)

1 garlic clove, crushed

1/4 cup parsley

1 tsp chilli flakes (or fresh chilli)

Sea salt and black pepper to taste

1. Combine avocado and beans in a food processor or mash by hand. Add a splash of extra virgin olive oil if desired.

2. Add the lemon juice, garlic, parsley, chilli, salt and pepper to the mash and set aside.

3. Bring a saucepan of water with vinegar and 1 tsp of salt to a boil over a medium heat.

4. Reduce to a simmer and stir the water clockwise to create a whirlpool.

5. One at a time crack the egg into the water, some people find it easier to crack the egg into a bowl first before adding to the saucepan.

6. Cook the egg for 2 – 3 minutes before removing with a slotted spoon.

7. Serve the eggs on top of the avocado bean mash.

TRIPLE BERRY
QUINOA PORRIDGE

This is a great recipe to use up leftover quinoa and is a different yet easy spin on the traditional oat porridge. The burst of flavours the berries offer is a welcome start to any day and the inclusion of cinnamon is a great blood sugar stabiliser to include in your daily diet.

(SERVES 1, MULTIPLY AS NEEDED)

³/₄ cup cooked quinoa

¹/₄ cup natural yoghurt (or coconut milk)

1 tbsp unsweetened shredded coconut

Pinch of cinnamon

Handful of blueberries, raspberries and blackberries

8 almonds (pre-soaked overnight and chopped)

1. In a bowl combine quinoa with yoghurt, shredded coconut and cinnamon to taste.

2. Top porridge with berries and chopped almonds.

3. If extra sweetness is desired add a sweetener of choice, either a small amount of local raw honey, rice malt syrup, stevia or a couple of dates.

SUMMER AVOCADO AND CUCUMBER SOUP WITH MINT RADISH SALSA

1 large cucumber

1 large avocado

1 cup chicken or vegetable stock (plus more as needed)

1 tbsp lemon juice

Salt and pepper to taste

3 radishes

$^1/_2$ tsp apple cider vinegar

1 tbsp finely chopped fresh mint

1. Peel, deseed and dice the cucumber, remove the skin from the avocado and add cucumber and avocado flesh to the bowl of a food processor.

2. Puree the cucumber and avocado while adding the chicken stock until you reach desired consistency. Add lemon juice and seasoning.

3. Prepare the salsa by finely dicing the radishes, adding apple cider vinegar and stirring through chopped mint.

4. Serve avocado and cucumber soup chilled with a spoonful of the mint radish salsa on top.

GREEN BREAKFAST SMOOTHIE

Breakfast is often a missed opportunity for many people to get a head start on their vegetable intake for the day. This recipe is not only loaded with nutritious greens but it's a quick and easy meal on the go for those racing out the door in the morning.

(SERVES 1)

1 cup of baby spinach (or kale, silver beet)

1 ripe banana (frozen for extra creaminess)

$1/_2$ an avocado

1 small Lebanese cucumber

$1/_2$-inch piece of fresh ginger root

$1^1/_2$ cups of water (almond milk or coconut water)

$1/_4$ cup of lemon juice (fresh)

Pinch of cinnamon

Handful of ice

1. Chop all ingredients up into similar sized chunks.

2. Combine spinach, banana, avocado, cucumber, ginger, water, lemon juice, cinnamon and ice in a blender and blend on high until smooth and creamy.

3. If more liquid is needed add in additional water a little at a time until desired consistency is reached.

BLACK FOREST SMOOTHIE

This quick and easy smoothie is great any time of the day with a slight sweetness from the cherries and depth of flavour thanks to the raw cacao. It makes one generous smoothie or two smaller smoothies to share.

1 small can of full fat coconut milk (approximately 270ml)

$1/_2$ cup frozen, pitted Morello cherries

1 tbsp raw cacao powder

$1/_4$ cup of shredded coconut

In a blender combine coconut milk, cherries, raw cacao powder and shredded coconut until smooth.

Soups, Salads and Sides

For many the idea of making a soup, salad or snack from scratch (as opposed to out of a tin or packet) is enough to send them into panic mode. We often forget that cooking doesn't come easily to a lot of people, and for many the prospect of hours in the kitchen just isn't worth the time or bother.

If cooking isn't high on your priority list then fear not, there are plenty of quick, cheap and easy ways to go homemade without the hassle. Soups and salads make easy meals that can be whipped up in little to no time, make large quantities, and can be eaten as leftovers, meaning you cook less in the long-run.

Depending on where you live in the world, supermarkets and up-market grocers cater at varying levels to our need for convenience as society becomes increasingly time poor. Ready-made meals may be sold as an easy option for busy individuals or may be wrapped in a "healthy" box for those wishing to lose weight without having to do much cooking themselves. Either way, a prepared, store-bought meal comes with more than what the cleverly crafted picture on the front of the box wants you to see, and a reading of the nutritional panel and ingredients list is a must.

Canned and dehydrated soup first appeared in the early 19th century primarily for military personnel, but of course varied widely from what you can expect to find on a supermarket shelf these days. Often with excess salt and sugar present, the humble can of soup is also home to preservatives, flavour enhancers and possible traces of Bisphenol A (BPA) in the lining of the can.

With a little preparation and forward thinking, you can avoid having to reach for a can of soup or a premade salad and whip up tasty and healthy versions of your own at home.

ROASTED BRUSSELS SPROUTS SALAD WITH TAHINI DRESSING

Even the fussiest eater will be surprised by the flavour that roasting brings out in these Brussels sprouts and the tahini dressing is so versatile, it's great drizzled over any salad.

250g Brussels sprouts

Olive oil

2 tsp chilli flakes (optional)

Salt and pepper to taste

Tahini dressing

2 tbsp hulled tahini

2 tbsp water (more as needed)

Zest and juice of ¹⁄₂ a lemon

1 tsp paprika

1 clove of garlic, crushed (optional)

1. Preheat the oven to 180°C/356°F and line an oven tray with baking paper.

2. Trim the ends from the Brussels sprouts before coating in olive oil, chilli flakes, salt and pepper. Roast for approximately 20 minutes until browned but not burned.

3. Prepare the dressing by whisking tahini, water, lemon zest, paprika and crushed garlic in a small bowl.

4. Serve the Brussels sprouts warm with the dressing over the top.

WARM CAULIFLOWER FATTOUSH SALAD

1 medium head of cauliflower, cut into florets

1 bunch of white (or red) radishes

3 celery stalks, cut into chunks

1 continental cucumber, cut into chunks

Extra virgin olive oil

1 tsp salt

1 tsp pepper

1 tbsp sumac

1 tsp ground coriander

Zest of 1 lemon

Pita crips

4 small rounds of pita bread

15 g butter

1 tbsp olive oil

1$\frac{1}{2}$ tsp salt

1 tbsp chilli flakes (optional)

1. Preheat oven to 180°C/356°F. Drizzle cauliflower and radishes with olive oil and roast for 15 minutes before adding the celery and cucumber. Roast for a further 10 minutes.

2. Prepare the spice mix in a small bowl, adding the lemon zest at the end. Set aside.

3. Prepare the pita crisps by melting the butter and oil in a frying pan or skillet. Tear the pita bread into chunks and add to the pan, turning each piece until coated and cooking for 5 minutes until crispy. Remove from the pan and sprinkle with salt and chilli flakes (if using).

4. Assemble the warm salad with cauliflower, radishes, cucumber and celery, sprinkle with the spice mix and pita crisps.

LEMON LENTIL SOUP

Soup needn't be an hours-long affair; this recipe can be started when you walk in the door after work and can be on the table 30 minutes later. Having homemade chicken or vegetable stock on hand helps but if you're not prepared then a good quality store-bought stock can be substituted, just be vigilant with label reading and remember you get what you pay for. Additional vegetables can be added but aim to use fast cooking ones such as zucchini or spinach, or steam the vegetables before adding to the soup.

4 celery stalks, thinly sliced

4 cups chicken or vegetable stock

1 cup red lentils

Zest and juice of ½ lemon

Sea salt and black pepper

½ cup parsley, finely chopped

1. Soften the celery stalks in a stock pot with a drizzle of olive oil.

2. Add the chicken or vegetable stock followed by the lentils.

3. Cook for 30 minutes, stirring occasionally unti lentils are coated.

4. Remove the soup from the heat and stir in the lemon zest, lemon juice, salt, pepper and parsley.

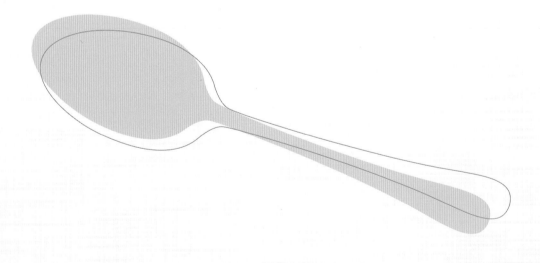

WARM SWEET POTATO AND KALE SALAD WITH GRAPEFRUIT DRESSING

2 cups kale

2 small/medium sweet potatoes

$^1/_2$ cup fresh grapefruit juice (approximately $^1/_2$ a medium sized grapefruit)

1 tbsp apple cider vinegar

$^1/_4$ tsp paprika

$^1/_4$ tsp hot mustard

1. Peel sweet potato and cut into evenly sized chunks. Steam until tender.

2. Roughly chop kale leaves and lightly steam. Combine in a bowl with sweet potato.

3. Prepare the dressing by whisking grapefruit juice with apple cider vinegar, paprika and hot mustard.

4. Pour dressing over the warm sweet potato and kale.

BEEF RICE PAPER ROLLS

(MAKES 6)

6 sheets of rice paper

300g cooked steak, thinly sliced (a great way to use up leftover meat from the previous night's dinner)

100g vermicelli noodles

½ carrot, cut into thin batons

2 spring onions, thinly sliced

Small wedge of red cabbage, finely sliced

Small wedge of green cabbage, finely sliced

Sauce

2 tbsp soy sauce

2 tsp sesame oil

Sesame seeds

1. Prepare steak, carrot, spring onion, red and green cabbage to have ready to go.

2. Soak vermicelli noodles per packet instructions in boiling water before draining and setting aside.

3. Pour warm water into a medium sized bowl. One at a time, dip the rice paper into the warm water for approximately 30 seconds until softened.

4. Place rice paper onto a damp tea towel and begin assembling.

5. Starting on one side of the rice paper, 2cm in from the edge, add a small amount of vermicelli noodles, sliced steak, carrot, spring onion, red and green cabbage.

6. Roll the rice paper forward, enclosing the filling, until half way along the sheet. Fold both sides in and continue rolling. If you've used too much filling you may have to remove some to roll it properly. If the end isn't sticking down, wet your finger with a little water and run it along the edge of the rice paper before pressing down to seal.

7. Repeat with remaining ingredients, store rolls in the refrigerator and serve with a dipping sauce of soy sauce and sesame oil mixed together. Sprinkle sesame seeds on top of sauce for extra crunch.

SOBA NOODLE SALAD WITH PRAWNS AND LIME DRESSING

25g soba noodles

6 raw prawn cutlets

4 asparagus spears

½ small red capsicum

1 spring onion

1 garlic clove

Wedge of lime

Salt and pepper to taste

1. Place noodles in a small bowl and pour over boiling water according to package instructions. After soaking for several minutes, drain and set aside.

2. Shave asparagus spears or finely slice, along with the red capsicum and spring onion.

3. Add a small amount of coconut oil to a hot pan before cooking the garlic; followed by the prawns until they're pink in colour. Add asparagus, capsicum and spring onion and stir-fry for a few minutes until just tender. Season with salt and pepper if desired.

4. Add the noodles to the pan and mix through before serving with lime juice squeezed over the top.

RATATOUILLE

A great side dish to accompany your protein of choice, ratatouille can be made following the method below or in a more rustic fashion by dicing the vegetables into chunks and roasting. Be careful to read the label when buying a pasata or tomato puree and always choose a product with no added sugar.

1 zucchini

1 small eggplant

1 red onion

2 tomatoes

1 cup passata (tomato puree)

1 tbsp dried oregano

1 tbsp dried basil

1. Preheat the oven to 190°C/375°F.

2. Pour tomato passata in the bottom of a shallow baking dish.

3. Using a mandolin or a knife, evenly slice the vegetables into discs and layer in alternating order over the tomato passata.

4. Brush the tops of the vegetables with olive oil and sprinkle the oregano and basil over the top.

5. Cover with baking paper and cook in the oven for approximately 40-50 minutes until all vegetables are tender.

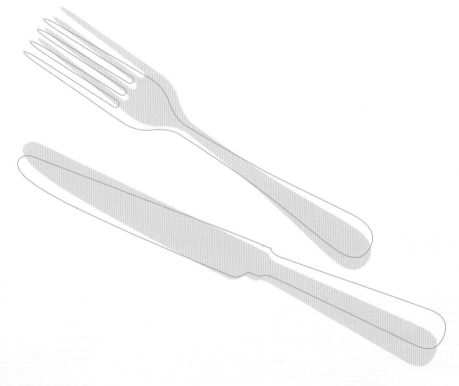

PUMPKIN AND SPINACH SOUP

300g pumpkin

2 tsp dried chilli flakes

2 tbsp coconut oil

4 cups chicken or vegetable stock

200g baby spinach

1 cup coconut milk

Salt and pepper to taste

1. Cut pumpkin into similar sized chunks and remove skin. Pour over coconut oil and dried chilli flakes and roast in the oven for 25-30 minutes or until tender.

2. In a saucepan combine chicken or vegetable stock, roasted pumpkin and baby spinach. Bring to a simmer before using a stick blender to puree. If you don't have a stick blender, let the mixture cool before processing it in a blender in batches.

3. Stir through coconut milk and season with salt and pepper.

Roasting the pumpkin before adding it to the stock and spinach adds an incredible depth of flavour. You can replace the chilli flakes with other spices if you want. Ginger, cumin, nutmeg or tumeric would also work well with the pumpkin and coconut flavours. You can also omit the coconut milk if you're happy with a thinner consistency.

Mains

"What's for dinner?" is a painful question for many, and the stress involved with creating interesting and flavourful meals seven days a week can wear a person down, especially if they have young mouths to feed. It's no surprise that we increasingly turn to convenient options come the end of the day, whether it's going through the drive through for a burger or ordering takeout to be delivered to our front door, even the option of reheating a frozen meal from the supermarket seems more appealing to some than whipping up a quick meal after work.

Often we'll turn to a jar of sauce or a packet of flavouring to add to our meals, making dinner that little bit easier to handle each night. Unfortunately this easy-to-make mistake can cost you big in the sugar department, especially if you're reaching for a jar of curry sauce or paste. A quick scan of the Asian sauce shelves at the supermarket showed me a jar of chicken korma sauce with 6.6g of sugar per 100g, and a jar of butter chicken sauce with 7.2g per 100g. If you wanted to add a little mango chutney to your dish that jar had 49.1g of sugar per 100g. In the mood for a yummy laksa tonight? A popular brand of laksa paste listed 13.4g of sugar per 100g. Just want to get some takeaway sushi for an easy meal? If the restaurant used Mirin seasoning on the rice it could have as much as 43.8g of sugar per 100g.

If thinking of what to cook for dinner brings on a headache, just remember there are quick and easy options for weeknights that'll have you in and out of the kitchen in under half an hour – with a little practice perhaps. Save the more elaborate meals and experiments for the weekend or holidays, and reduce the stress you associate with a meal that should be enjoyed around the table with friends and family, discussing the events of the day.

FISH CAKES WITH CHILLI HUMMUS

You can use any type of fish you like here; this recipe makes about 6 small cakes. You could also replaced the fish with minced chicken or use leftover quinoa. If adjusting the recipe you may need to add additional eggs or breadcrumbs to make the mixture stick together. Make your own breadcrumbs using a stale baguette that you grind into crumbs using a food processor or stick blender. If you'd prefer the breadcrumbs can be replaced with almond meal or the cakes can be left uncoated.

120g salmon, minced

1 egg

1 tbsp chopped dill

½ cup fresh breadcrumbs

Sea salt and black pepper to taste

400g cooked chickpeas (from a tin is fine)

2 tbsp hulled tahini

Juice of half a lemon

¼ cup dried chilli flakes (or more if you want it extra spicy)

100ml extra virgin olive oil

Salt and pepper to taste

In the bowl of a food processor mince the fish fillets before adding egg, dill, salt and pepper.

Sprinkle breadcrumbs over a plate and take small handfuls of the salmon paste and roll into balls.

Coat each ball in breadcrumbs and press down gently to flatten.

Heat some coconut oil in a pan and shallow fry the cakes until golden and the fish is just cooked, approximately 4-5 minutes. Cut one cake open to check it is cooked.

Using a stick blender or food processor, combine chickpeas, tahini, lemon juice and chilli flakes. Slowly add the olive oil and blend to desired consistency, seasoning with salt and pepper. You may want to add more lemon juice or olive oil as you go depending on flavour and thickness of the hummus.

SPEEDY EGGPLANT & SPINACH CURRY

Usually whipping up a curry involves using a store bought jar of sauce or curry paste, full of excess salt and hidden sugar. The alternative is to make your own curry paste, which is not ideal for a weeknight when you just want dinner on the table quickly. This curry doesn't compromise on taste but is simple and speedy, making it a recipe you'll want to come back to week after week.

1 onion, diced

Extra virgin olive oil

350g baby spinach leaves

1 medium eggplant, diced

1-inch piece of ginger, grated

1 tsp ground cumin

1 tsp ground turmeric

1 tsp ground coriander

270ml coconut milk

1 can of chickpeas

1. In a medium saucepan, soften the onion in olive oil before adding the spinach and wilting.

2. Add the eggplant, ginger, cumin, turmeric and coriander and cook for 5 minutes before adding the coconut milk and chickpeas.

3. Cook for 10 - 15 minutes until the eggplant is cooked.

4. Serve with rice or on its own.

RICOTTA GNOCCHI WITH ZUCCHINI AND FENNEL SAUCE

Ricotta gnocchi

250g ricotta

1 egg yolk

1 tsp salt

½ cup plain flour (plus extra for dusting)

1. In a small bowl whisk egg yolk and salt before folding in the ricotta.

2. Using a spoon slowly stir in the flour, being careful not to overwork the mixture.

3. Sprinkle some flour on your work surface and working with a handful of the dough at a time, gently roll starting from the middle and moving out until you have a long sausage. If the mixture gets stuck on the work surface simply sprinkle a little more flour over it. Use a knife to cut the sausage into small segments and place on a tray or board lined with baking paper. Repeat with the remaining dough.

4. Bring a large pot of salted water to a boil while you prepare the sauce.

5. Once the water has come to a boil add the gnocchi and cook until they come to the surface.

Zucchini and fennel sauce

1 large zucchini

½ a bulb of fennel

30g butter, cubed

1 tsp ground paprika

1 tsp ground nutmeg

Salt and pepper to taste

1. Slice the zucchini and fennel into thin strips.

2. Heat a fry pan and melt the butter before adding the zucchini, fennel, paprika, nutmeg, salt and pepper. Cook until softened.

3. Remove gnocchi from the pot with a slotted spoon and add to the pan of sauce. Gently stir gnocchi through the sauce before serving.

STUFFED LAMB MINCE PEPPERS

(SERVES 2)

2 large peppers (capsicum), any colour

¹/₂ brown onion, diced

¹/₂ large zucchini, shredded

¹/₂ medium carrot, shredded

250g lamb mince

1 tsp dried mint

1 tbsp dried oregano

Salt and pepper to taste

Handful of parsley, roughly chopped

1. Preheat oven to 180°/356 °C.

2. Remove the core of each pepper ready for stuffing. Cut each pepper in half vertically through the core.

3. Drizzle peppers with a splash of extra virgin olive oil and roast in the oven for 15 minutes or until soft but still holding its shape.

4. Add a splash of extra virgin olive oil to a fry pan and cook onion until just translucent. Add lamb mince, use a spoon to break up any lumps and cook until browned. Add seasonings and cook for a further 5 minutes before tasting and adjusting flavour if needed.

5. Stir through shredded zucchini and carrot and cook for 3 – 4 minutes.

6. Fill each pepper with the mince stuffing and top with roughly chopped parsley.

CHICKEN COLESLAW

It's tempting to pay a visit to the condiments aisle at the supermarket for a cheap and easy coleslaw dressing but a quick survey of the ingredients list and you'll discover you're paying more in the long run when you entrust your health to the big companies. It's incredibly easy to make delicious dressings and sauces at home without the excess sugar and salt.

(SERVES 2)

2 chicken breast fillets, skin removed

2 tbsp lemon juice

¼ red cabbage, thinly sliced

¼ green cabbage, thinly sliced

1 red capsicum, deseeded and thinly sliced

1 green capsicum, deseeded and thinly sliced

1 carrot, skin washed (but not peeled) and thinly sliced

2 spring onions (green onions), chopped

½ cup of coriander (cilantro)

Dressing

2 tbsp extra virgin olive oil

4 tbsp apple cider vinegar

1 tsp sesame oil

1 tbsp Dijon mustard (or wholegrain)

1-inch piece of fresh ginger, grated

Sea salt and black pepper

Fresh chilli (optional)

1. Bring a small saucepan of water with a pinch of salt and 2 tbsp of lemon juice to a boil and add the chicken breasts, immediately reducing the heat to a simmer.

2. Poach the chicken breasts for approximately 10 – 15 minutes, depending on the size of the fillets. Use a thermometer to test that the chicken has reached the minimum safe temperature of 75°C or 170°F.

3. Leave the chicken to cool before slicing or shredding.

4. Combine the thinly sliced vegetables, except for the spring onion and coriander, in a bowl. Add the cooled poached chicken.

5. In a small bowl whisk the extra virgin olive oil, apple cider vinegar, sesame oil, mustard, grated ginger, salt and pepper.

6. Pour dressing over coleslaw and chicken and toss to combine. Garnish with coriander and spring onion.

ZUCCHINI, LEEK AND COTTAGE CHEESE FRITTATA WITH BASIL PESTO

This is a great recipe to make on the weekend and then divide into portions for the week ahead. You can substitute ricotta or feta for the cottage cheese, and can use any vegetables you have on hand. Serve on its own or with a side salad. With a stack of these sitting in the fridge you'll never be left wondering what's for lunch again!

(SERVES 4)

1 tbsp extra virgin olive oil

2 cloves of garlic, crushed

2 small zucchinis, diced

1 medium leek, white part only, thinly sliced

$1/2$ cup cottage cheese

8 free range eggs

Parsley, chopped

Sea salt and black pepper to taste

Basil pesto

$1/4$ cup almonds, pre-soaked overnight

2 cups of basil leaves

2 garlic cloves, crushed

$1/2$ cup of extra virgin olive oil

1. Pre-heat the oven to 200°C/392°F.

2. In an ovenproof pan (such as a cast iron skillet) over a medium heat, add the oil and sweat the garlic, zucchini and leek for approximately 10 minutes.

3. In a bowl whisk the eggs and parsley together before folding in the cottage cheese. Add salt and pepper if desired.

4. Remove the pan from the heat and add the egg mixture, taking care to spread it evenly around the zucchini and leek.

5. Place the pan in the oven and cook for 15 minutes until the frittata is golden brown.

6. While the frittata is cooking make the pesto by processing almonds, basil leaves, garlic and extra virgin olive oil together in a food processor.

7. Remove the frittata from the oven, slice and serve with a drizzle of the basil pesto on top.

ROASTED VEGETABLE STACKS WITH BLACK BEANS AND LEMON HUMMUS

The simplest meals are often the tastiest and in these roasted vegetable stacks the true flavours of the fresh produce are allowed to shine through. The lemon hummus gives an added zing but the vegetables would be just as tasty without it. Use vegetables that are in season in your local area or use what you have on hand in the fridge.

(SERVES 2)

1 can of black or kidney beans

1 eggplant

1 red onion

1 red capsicum

2 large Portobello mushrooms

2 zucchinis

2 garlic cloves, crushed

1 tbsp ground cumin

Extra virgin olive oil or coconut oil, enough to coat vegetables

Sea salt and black pepper to taste

Parsley, finely chopped

Lemon hummus

1 can (400g/14oz) of chickpeas

2 tbsp tahini, hulled or unhulled

3 tbsp fresh lemon juice

1 tbsp lemon zest

1 garlic clove, crushed

100 ml extra virgin olive oil

Sea salt and black pepper if needed

1. Preheat the oven to 200°C/392°F and prepare an oven tray with baking paper.

2. Cut the vegetables into equal sized slices, aim for 1-inch and keep consistent for even cooking. Keep the mushrooms whole but remove the stem.

3. Place vegetables into a bowl with garlic, cumin, salt, pepper and oil and mix well.

4. Place marinated vegetables onto prepared tray and roast in the oven until tender, approximately 30 minutes. Keep an eye on the mushrooms and remove from the oven earlier if necessary.

5. For the lemon hummus, drain the chickpeas and add to the bowl of a food processor.

6. Add tahini, garlic, lemon juice and zest.

7. Process until smooth; slowly adding the oilive oil. Taste and add salt or pepper if necessary.

8. Rinse the beans and either warm up in a small pan or leave at room temperature.

9. Beginning with the mushrooms, layer the vegetables, beans and lemon hummus on two plates and garnish with parsley.

SPICED BROCCOLI, KALE AND LENTIL BOWLS

Spice up your evening with this simple dish that takes only minutes to prepare. Using minimal ingredients, this recipe is one to have on hand for those nights when cooking feels like a chore. For a twist on this recipe, add half a cup of coconut milk after heating the spices to create a cheat's curry.

1 head of broccoli (including stem), cut into small chunks

1½ cups of kale, roughly chopped

1 can of lentils

2 tbsp coconut oil

2 tbsp natural yoghurt

Lemon zest

¼ cup of walnut pieces (optional)

Spice mix

½ tsp ground cumin

½ tsp chilli flakes (or fresh chilli)

¼ tsp cinnamon

¼ tsp ground coriander

¼ tsp ground fenugreek (optional)

Sea salt

1 garlic clove, crushed

1-inch piece of fresh ginger, grated

1. Combine spices in a bowl.

2. Lightly steam broccoli and kale and set aside.

3. Drain the lentils and rinse thoroughly under water.

4. In a pan over medium heat add the oil and spice mix, cooking gently to release the aromas.

5. Add the broccoli, kale and lentils and coat with the spices. Heat through.

6. Serve the spiced broccoli, kale and lentils with a dollop of natural yoghurt, lemon zest and walnuts on top.

Desserts and Snacks

Now we come to the recipe section that has most people intrigued – how do you lead a Low Sugar No Sugar lifestyle and still enjoy desserts and snacks? Can you really still enjoy a slice of cheesecake or chocolate if you're cutting out or reducing fructose from your diet?

Firstly you need to remember why you have decided to embark on a Low Sugar No Sugar lifestyle. You can't reduce the amount of sugar in your diet and still expect to eat sweet desserts all the time. You need to update your way of thinking and remember it's not that you *can't* have cake and chocolate and lollies, it's that you don't *want* to. There are plenty of ways to enjoy sweet treats without excess fructose and processed sugar but ultimately when you wave goodbye to conventional desserts you're also farewelling their level of sweetness and overall texture.

The following desserts range from quick and easy to the more complex, offering you ideas for those days when you want something sweet fast, and recipes for the times when you want a little more of a challenge. They also range in sweetness, from some with no more than a tablespoon of a sweetener such as rice malt syrup, to the banana caramel cake or wagon wheel slice that use more and should be shared.

Once you've started reducing the amount of sweetness in your diet you may want to adjust the following recipes to your taste. I have used a mixture of safe sweeteners and different types of flours to make the following recipes more widely appealing but you can certainly substitute your sweetener of choice, switching out dextrose for stevia etc.

The key to making (and enjoying) desserts and sticking to a Low Sugar No Sugar lifestyle is always moderation. Replacing refined white sugar with dextrose, stevia, rice malt syrup or fruit is not a free license to eat something from this section every day. Common sense still prevails and dessert should remain an occasional treat.

ORANGE & POPPY SEED TRUFFLES

This treat combines tartness and sweetness with the familiar flavour pairing of orange and poppyseed. Truffles are traditionally made from chocolate and cream, with healthier recipes subbing in nuts and dates, amongst other things. The use of ricotta in a truffle may perplex some, but once you retrain your tastebuds to recognise, and appreciate, more than just the sweetness in food these cheesecake balls will delight.

200g firm ricotta cheese

2 tbsp rice malt syrup

Zest of 1 orange

Zest of ½ lemon

1 tbsp poppy seeds

Optional coatings: raw cacao, shredded coconut, crushed nuts etc.

1. Mix ricotta with rice malt syrup, orange and lemon zest, and poppy seeds. Stir to combine and remove large lumps but don't over mix and soften the ricotta too much.

2. Place bowl in the refrigerator for 15 minutes to firm up.

3. Choose your coating of choice and sprinkle it onto a plate.

4. Take small spoonfuls of the mixture and roll into equal-sized balls in your hands.

5. Roll each ball in a coating and store in an airtight container in the refrigerator.

CHOC-AVO PROFITEROLES

Profiteroles

1 cup water

80g butter, chopped

1 cup rice flour

3 free range eggs, whisked

Choc-avo filling

1 avocado

4 tbsp raw cacao

2 tbsp raw honey or
rice malt syrup

1. Pre-heat oven to 200°C/392°F.

2. In a small saucepan melt the butter with the water and bring to a boil.

3. Remove pan from the heat and add the flour, using a spoon to stir until the mixture forms a ball and comes away from the side of the pan. Leave to cool for 2 - 3 minutes.

4. Add one egg at a time, mixing between additions until the mixture is glossy.

5. Using a spoon or piping bag, evenly divide the mixture onto a parchment-lined oven tray. The neater you are at this stage, the rounder the profiteroles will be after cooking.

6. As an optional extra, brush the top of each profiterole with a dab of milk or whisked egg.

7. Bake in the oven for 25 - 30 minutes until puffed. Turn the oven off; remove the tray and using a skewer poke a small hole in each profiterole to release steam.

8. Return the tray to the oven while the oven is cooling down, leaving the oven door ajar.

9. While the profiteroles are cooling make the choc-avo filling. In a food processor add the avocado flesh and pulse until smooth and creamy. Add the cacao and raw honey and pulse to combine.

10. Once profiteroles are room temperature, either pipe the choc-avo filling into each through a small hole in the base or slice each profiterole in half and spoon the mixture into the bottom half, add a strawberry (or other fruit) segment and top with the profiterole lid.

STRAWBERRY CHEESECAKE

This is one of my favourite Low Sugar No Sugar recipes because it surprises so many people who think lowering the amount of sugar in their diet means they have to go without their favourite dessert. This cheesecake is so smooth and creamy it's hard to stop at one slice. It uses the same base recipe as the Wagon Wheel Slice so once you make either recipe you've already mastered part of a second LSNS dessert recipe!

Almond shortbread base

1½ cups plain flour

1 cup almond meal

Pinch of salt

¼ cup dextrose

1 tsp vanilla powder

180g butter, cubed

¼ cup water

1. Preheat the oven to 160°C/320°F.

2. Sift flour, almond meal, salt, dextrose and vanilla powder in a bowl.

3. Add the cubed butter and using your fingers work it through the flour like you would a crumble mixture until evenly distributed, some lumps are okay.

4. Add the water and form the dough into a ball.

5. Wrap in cling film and refrigerate for 10 - 15 minutes.

6. Remove the dough from the fridge and press into the base of a 20cm spring form tin lined with baking paper.

7. Bake in the oven for 15 - 20 minutes or until golden brown and a skewer comes out clean, careful not to burn it.

Filling

400g strawberries

1 tbsp gelatine

500g cream cheese

$\frac{1}{2}$ cup rice malt syrup

1 tsp vanilla powder

250ml double cream

1. Hull the strawberries, clean and place in the bowl of a food processor. Blend until smooth then push through a sieve to remove the seeds. You can keep the seeds in but removing them will help create an ultra smooth cheesecake.

2. Place the strawberry puree in a small saucepan over a low heat. Sprinkle the gelatine over the top and stir to combine. Heat the mixture until the strawberry puree has thickened, 3 – 5 minutes. Remove from heat and let cool.

3. Beat the cream cheese until smooth and lump free.

4. Add the rice malt syrup and vanilla powder.

5. Fold in the strawberry puree followed by the double cream until just combined.

6. Pour mixture over the cheesecake base and refrigerate overnight.

WAGON WHEEL SLICE

This recipe has the most steps of any LSNS recipe but trust me when I say it's worth it. It came about one day when I had a craving for an Australian childhood favourite treat, the Wagon Wheel biscuit. When I broke down the components I realised it would be quite easy to substitute the refined sugar for a low-fructose friendly alternative, and the Wagon Wheel Slice was born. This recipe serves to demonstrate how with a little imagination, you can take your favourite desserts or supermarket products and put your own Low Sugar No Sugar spin on it.

Almond shortbread base

1½ cups plain flour

1 cup almond meal

Pinch of salt

¼ cup dextrose

1 tsp vanilla powder

180g butter, cubed

¼ cup water

1. Preheat the oven to 160°C/320°F.

2. Sift flour, almond meal, salt, dextrose and vanilla powder in a bowl.

3. Add the cubed butter and using your fingers work it through the flour like you would a crumble mixture until evenly distributed, some lumps are okay.

4. Add the water and form the dough into a ball.

5. Wrap in cling film and refrigerate for 10 - 15 minutes.

6. Remove the dough from the fridge and press into the base of a lined baking tray, the size of which will determine the thickness of the biscuit. For a thicker base use a small brownie pan, for a thinner base use a larger pan.

7. Bake in the oven for 20 minutes until golden brown and a skewer comes out clean. If making a thinner base check it between 10 - 15 minutes and be careful not to burn it.

Strawberry-Raspberry Jam

1 cup strawberries, fresh or frozen

1 cup raspberries, fresh or frozen

1 tbsp water

½ tbsp gelatin

1. In a small pan heat strawberries, raspberries and water until the berries break down, keep as chunky as you like.

2. Remove pan from heat and add gelatin, stirring to dissolve.

3. Set the mixture to the side while you make the marshmallow.

Marshmallow

½ cup water

1½ tbsp gelatine

½ cup rice malt syrup

½ tsp vanilla extract

⅛ tsp salt

1. In a small bowl combine ¼ cup of water with the gelatine. You can use either a hand or stand mixer for this recipe, both with the whisk attachment. If using a stand mixer, combine water and gelatine in the mixer's standard bowl, ready for step #3.

2. In a small saucepan combine ¼ cup of water with the rice malt syrup and salt and bring to a boil over medium heat. Using a candy thermometer bring the mixture to soft ball point or 118°C/244°F.

3. Remove from heat and slowly pour the rice malt syrup mixture into the gelatine mixture from step #1, with the mixer on slow. Whisk for approximately 10 minutes until white and fluffy.

4. Immediately pour the marshmallow mixture over the short-bread base before it begins to set. If it has started to set, gently reheat the mixture to loosen it.

5. Pour the strawberry-raspberry jam over the top of the marshmallow layer and refrigerate for 10 minutes.

Chocolate topping

½ cup cacao butter

1 tbsp rice malt syrup

3 tbsp raw cacao

1. In a small pan melt the cacao butter and rice malt syrup.

2. Add the cacao, stir and bring the mixture to 48°C/118°F. Remove from heat and let cool for 3 minutes.

3. Remove the slice from the fridge and pour on the chocolate topping. Use either a palette knife to spread the chocolate or gently turn the pan to spread the chocolate.

4. Return the slice to the fridge for at least one hour before slicing and enjoying. Store in the refrigerator.

You can find good quality cacao butter and raw cacao at health food stores, speciality grocers and online.

BANANA CARAMEL CAKE

(MAKES 2 SMALL BUNDT CAKES OR 1 LARGE CAKE)

Banana Cake

100g butter, cubed

¹/₂ cup dextrose

2 free range eggs

**¹/₃ cup coconut water
(or plain water)**

³/₄ cup rice flour

**¹/₃ cup wholemeal spelt
flour**

¹/₄ tsp baking powder

2 bananas

Caramel Sauce

10g butter, cubed

¹/₂ cup dextrose

2 tbsp water

¹/₂ cup cream

1. Preheat oven to 180°C/356°F.

2. Using a hand mixer or a freestanding mixer, cream the butter and dextrose until light and fluffy.

3. Add eggs one at a time until just combined.

4. In a separate bowl, sift flour and baking powder together.

5. Add half the coconut water and half the flour to the butter mixture and beat until combined. Add the remaining half and beat to combine.

6. Mash the bananas and add to the mixture.

7. Divide batter between two small baking moulds or pour into one large pan. Bake in the oven for 45 minutes to 1 hour, testing with a skewer to check if the batter is cooked. Remove from oven and cool on a wire rack before turning out of pans.

8. Prepare the caramel sauce by melting the butter, dextrose and water in a small pan for 5 minutes until it comes to a boil. Remove from the heat and add the cream, stirring to combine until it thickens. Set aside to cool.

9. Serve the cakes plain or with caramel sauce poured over the top.

NUTTY FUDGE BITES

**1 cup pecan nut butter
(or substitute with any
nut butter)**

$^1/_2$ cup coconut oil

1 tbsp rice malt syrup

$^1/_2$ cup raw cacao

$^1/_2$ cup macadamia nuts

1. Melt coconut oil and add to a bowl with nut butter, rice malt syrup and raw cacao. Stir until combined, whisk if necessary to remove any large lumps.

2. Roughly chop macadamia nuts and fold through the mixture.

3. Spoon fudge into 12 mini cupcake liners and refrigerate for 30 minutes. Store in the refrigerator.

*Alternatively pour fudge mixture into a lined shallow baking tin, refrigerate and then slice into squares.

TART BLUEBERRY MACAROON POTS

More tart than sweet, this dessert is perfect for those wanting something to end a meal that satisfies but doesn't send their blood sugar levels soaring.

Macaroon Crumb

1 egg white

1 tbsp rice malt syrup

Pinch of salt

$^2/_3$ cup shredded coconut

1. Preheat oven to 180°C/356°F.

2. Whisk egg white, rice malt syrup and salt in a small bowl until frothy. Stir through shredded coconut.

3. Pour mixture onto an oven tray lined with baking paper.

4. Bake approximately 15 minutes until golden in colour.

5. Remove from oven and set aside to cool.

Blueberry filling

250g blueberries (if using frozen berries thaw before using)

50g goat's cheese

$^1/_2$ cup sour cream

$^1/_4$ tsp vanilla powder

1. Whisk goat's cheese, sour cream and vanilla powder in a bowl.

2. Fold through blueberries

3. Assemble the pots by spooning the blueberry mixture evenly between four small bowls.

4. Top each bowl with macaroon crumbs and set in the refrigerator for at least 1 hour.

Vanilla powder is available at health food stores, speciality grocers and online. It's usually twice the price of vanilla extract but a little goes a long way so is cheaper in the long run.

UPSIDE DOWN CHOCOLATE PISTACHIO CHEESECAKE

This crustless cheesecake removes the traditional sweet biscuit base found in most recipes. It's called an upside-down cheesecake because the nuts, which many healthier recipes replace a biscuit base with, appear on top rather than underneath the filling. The problem with using nuts as a "healthy" replacement is that often the amount we use exceeds the amount we should actually be eating daily. By placing the nuts on top of the cake you can monitor how much you're consuming; the 85g listed in the ingredients is a guide and can be reduced for personal preference or allergies. Because the cheesecake is crust-less it's extremely important that you line the base and sides of a spring form tin with baking paper. It's also important to refrigerate the cheesecake overnight to firm the mixture up. For a twist on this recipe use cupcake liners to make individual portions; fill as you would the larger tin, top with a spoon of the chocolate sauce and a sprinkling of pistachios.

Filling

¹⁄₃ cup raw cacao powder

50g dark chocolate (minimum 70%)

¹⁄₄ cup coconut milk

1 tbsp gelatine

500g cream cheese

¹⁄₂ cup rice malt syrup

1 tsp vanilla powder

250ml double cream

Chocolate topping

¹⁄₂ cup cacao butter

1 tbsp rice malt syrup

3 tbsp raw cacao

Crust

85g shelled pistachios

Pinch of sea salt

1. Line the base and sides of a spring form tin with baking paper.

2. In a small saucepan over low heat combine raw cacao, dark chocolate and coconut milk. Once melted, sprinkle the gelatine over the top and stir to combine. Heat the mixture until thickened, 3 – 5 minutes. Remove from heat and let cool.

3. Beat the cream cheese until smooth and lump free.

4. Add the rice malt syrup and vanilla powder.

5. Fold in cacao mixture followed by the double cream until just combined.

6. Pour mixture into the spring form tin and refrigerate overnight.

7. Prepare the chocolate topping by melting cacao butter, rice malt syrup and raw cacao in a small saucepan. Allow to cool before pouring over the top of the cheesecake and tilting the tin to spread the mixture evenly. Return to the refrigerator for 15 minutes.

8. Finely chop the pistachios by hand or use a hand held mixer with the blade attachment. Stir through the salt and sprinkle pistachios over the top of the cheesecake before serving.

SPEEDY SINGLE SERVE CHOCOLATE PUDDING

²/₃ cup coconut milk solids*

1 tbsp rice malt syrup

1 tbsp raw cacao powder

Combine coconut milk, rice malt syrup and cacao in a bowl and whisk together. Simple as that. Top with nuts of your choice or eat plain.

* Depending on the coconut milk brand you use and your climate, you'll usually find enough solids in the top of a 270ml can of coconut milk to make this recipe. If you don't have enough, drain half the liquid (and reserve for another recipe) and place the remaining half of the liquid and the solids into a bowl in the fridge. Chill for an hour and whisk.

CHILLI POPCORN

1/3 **cup popcorn kernels**

1 tsp coconut oil

1 tbsp chilli flakes

1 tsp cayenne pepper*

1/2 **tsp sea salt flakes**

1. Combine popcorn kernels, coconut oil, cayenne pepper and sea salt flakes in a brown paper bag. Fold down the top of the bag tightly, if not folded tight enough the popcorn will spill out of the bag while cooking.

2. Microwave on high for 2 minutes or until kernels stop popping. If there is a large amount of unpopped kernels after 2 minutes, return to the microwave and cook in 30 second bursts.

3. Enjoy warm or divide into containers or zip lock bags for work or school snacks.

* Add as much or as little chilli as you like/can handle. You can substitute the chilli with cinnamon, cumin or paprika, or try your own flavour combinations.

CHEDDAR AND ROSEMARY SCONES WITH PEPITA BUTTER

2 cups of self raising flour

125g cold butter, cubed

2 tsp salt

2 eggs

½ cup milk

1 cup cheddar cheese, shredded

2 tbsp fresh rosemary, finely chopped

1 egg white

Ground black pepper

1 cup pepitas (pumpkin seeds)

⅓ cup coconut oil, melted (plus more if needed)

1 tsp sea salt

1. Preheat the oven to 200°C/392°F.

2. Sift flour into the bowl of a stand mixer and add cubed butter. Using your hands, work the butter through the flour to make a crumble mixture.

3. Using the dough hook attachment set the mixer to a low speed and add salt, eggs, milk, cheese and rosemary. Work the dough until it forms a ball and comes away from the sides of the bowl.

4. Lightly flour a chopping board or work surface and turn the dough out onto it.

5. Roll or pat the dough out into a disc shape and use a round cookie cutter to cut scones out. Place each scone on a baking paper lined oven tray.

6. Whisk the egg white and brush the top of each scone with the wash before cracking some black pepper over the top.

7. Bake in the oven for approximately 15 minutes until golden brown on top. Cut one scone open to check the dough has cooked through.

8. While the scones are baking, place pepitas in the bowl of a food processor and blend on high until a butter mixture forms. The time it takes will depend on the mixer you have. The pepitas will form a crumb then a ball before finally hitting the butter stage.

9. Slowly add the coconut oil in through the feed tube to help the mixture along and season with sea salt.

Note: You can make the scones without a stand mixer, just knead the dough by hand and be prepared to use a little elbow grease.

For the Kids

Children have been fussy eaters for generations, causing their parents grief and refusing to eat certain things for no apparent reason. Often when a child is of school age their appetite is dictated by the breaks they're allocated during the day. Presuming they start with breakfast in the morning, once they get to school they get a recess, usually a short 15-20 minute break, followed by a 45 minute lunch break later in the day. After school the munchies can kick in around 3.30-4.00pm, then dinner around 6.30pm and maybe a dessert afterwards if they're lucky. That's a lot of opportunities to make less than desirable food choices.

Snacks were once small meals, often made from leftovers, and could include cuts of meat, vegetables, nuts and fruit. Nowadays they're seen more as convenience foods, low in nutritional value and bought cheaply and in bulk. Supermarket shelves are stacked full of cleverly marketed products designed to help make mum and dad's job a little easier, and to coerce impressionable children into asking for them.

The humble muesli bar now takes up multiple shelves, cleverly positioned next to the boxes of fruit juice for ease of shopping. A quick look at the nutritional panel on the back of the box shows you that some brands have as much sugar as a small chocolate bar, and I'm sure we both know which one most children would prefer. One box is labelled "fruit free" but still packs 15.5g of sugar per 100g. Another plasters the world "natural" all over the packaging and has 20g of sugar per 100g. A further box boasts "no artificial flavours or colourings" but has 29.1g of sugar per 100g.

With both parents usually working and the family budget often an issue, it's understandable why mum and dad turn to convenient foods when feeding the kids. While it may be a work in progress, and not as easy as it is for just you to change to a Low Sugar No Sugar lifestyle, there are a few simple recipes that can be substituted to help wean children off processed foods and into the LSNS mindset.

ZOODLES N'CHEESE

SERVES 1, MULTIPLY THE RECIPE ACCORDINGLY

1 zucchini

20g butter, cubed

¼ cup rice flour

¾ cup milk (or almond milk)

¼ cup shredded mozzarella or cheddar cheese

2 tbsp breadcrumbs

Salt and pepper to taste

1. Using a spiral cutter, julienne peeler or a regular vegetable peeler, slice the zucchini into "noodles". Place in a bowl and cover with boiling water for 4-5 minutes to cook. Alternatively, steam until just tender.

2. In a small saucepan, melt the butter before adding the rice flour to create a roux. Slowly whisk in the milk until the mixture thickens.

3. Stir in the shredded cheese and salt and pepper to taste.

4. In a small saucepan, dry toast the breadcrumbs until golden brown.

5. Pile the zoodles onto a plate and pour the cheese sauce over the top, garnishing with breadcrumbs.

PEPITA CRUSTED CHICKEN STRIPS

MAKES 12

400g chicken breast fillets

1 cup pepitas (pumpkin seeds)

1 cup plain flour

2 free range eggs

Sea salt

Optional extras: ¼ cup grated parmesan, 2 tbsp dried basil

1. Preheat the oven to 180°C/356°F.

2. Using a food processor or stick blender, blitz the pepitas until crushed. Spread over a plate.

3. On another plate sprinkle the flour. Crack 2 eggs into a bowl and whisk with a fork. (If using additional seasonings, add to the flour mixture before spreading on the plate.)

4. Slice the chicken breast fillets into strips.

5. Dip each strip into the flour followed by the egg and finally the crushed pepitas.

6. Place each strip on a baking paper lined oven tray before sprinkling a pinch of salt over the top.

7. Bake for 30 minutes, testing one strip to check the chicken is cooked before removing.

8. Serve with low sugar tomato sauce (page 52) or on their own.

SWEET POTATO NUGGETS

2 medium sweet potatoes

²/₃ cup shredded cheddar cheese

2 tsp sea salt

2 tsp paprika

Breadcrumbs or almond meal

1. Preheat the oven to 180°C/356°F.

2. Peel sweet potatoes, cut into equal sized chunks and steam.

3. Using a food processor or stick blender, puree sweet potato.

4. Add salt and paprika, then stir through cheddar cheese.

5. Sprinkle breadcrumbs or almond meal over a plate.

6. Using a spoon to measure out nuggets and keep at a uniform size. Roll handfuls of the mixture between your hands then press down gently to form a nugget shape.

7. Roll each nugget in the breadcrumbs before placing on a baking paper lined oven tray. The sweet potato should be sticky enough for the breadcrumbs to adhere to and will form a light coating.

8. Once you've rolled out all the mixture and lined them up on a baking tray, switch the oven on to grill, lightly spray each nugget with olive oil or brush with olive or coconut oil. Grill for 5 minutes or until golden brown before turning the nuggets over, spraying lightly with oil again and toasting the other side.

9. Serve with low sugar tomato sauce (page 52).

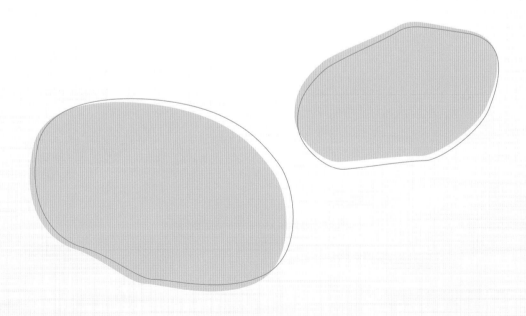

COTTAGE CHEESE PIKELETS

**2 cups rice flour
(can substitute with all
purpose flour)**

1 tsp baking powder

$\frac{1}{2}$ tsp salt

Zest of $\frac{1}{2}$ lemon

1 egg

1 cup milk

2 tbsp rice malt syrup

$\frac{1}{2}$ cup cottage cheese

1 tbsp lemon juice

Coconut oil

1. Sift flour and baking powder in a bowl, stir in salt and lemon zest.

2. Make a well in the centre and add egg, milk and rice malt syrup, stir to combine.

3. Stir through cottage cheese and lemon juice.

4. Add a couple of tablespoons of coconut oil to a pan and when hot drop spoonfuls of the mixture in. Wait until bubbles appear over the surface, flip and cook for a couple of minutes on the other side.

5. Serve with lemon juice drizzled over the top and fresh fruit if desired.

Note: Kids might need a little more encouragement to move away from the traditional sweet pancake so feel free to add more sweetener to begin with and slowly lower the amount the more times you make them.

Pancakes and pikelets are favourites for many kids but often contain sugar and are then covered in sugary toppings. Store-bought pancake mixes are popular because you only need to add an egg or some oil but on average contain 15g of sugar per 100g. It may take some getting used to but try substituting more savoury pancakes into your routine and slowly decreasing the frequency of sweeter breakfasts.

RASPBERRY FIZZ

Great for kids as an alternative to commercial red cordial or soft drinks, it may take some time to wean children off the excessively sweet store-bought variety but they'll come around eventually, and this raspberry fizz is far more satisfying.

1 cup of fresh or frozen raspberries

$^1/_2$ cup water

$^1/_2$ cup dextrose or $^3/_4$ tsp stevia

Sparkling water

1. Puree raspberries in a food processor or blender and set aside.

2. In a small saucepan combine water and dextrose and heat until dissolved.

3. Combine raspberry puree and liquid together before straining through a fine sieve to remove any remaining seeds.

4. Evenly distribute raspberry syrup between 4 – 6 glasses and top up with sparkling water.

CHOCOLATE CRACKLES

(MAKES 12)

2 cups puffed brown rice

½ cup unsweetened shredded coconut

½ cup dextrose or ¾ tsp stevia

½ cup virgin coconut oil

3 tbsp raw cacao

1. Combine puffed rice, coconut and dextrose in a bowl.

2. In a small saucepan melt the coconut oil (if solid) and cacao to form a chocolate sauce. Remove from heat and let cool for 2-3 minutes.

3. Pour chocolate mixture over the puffed rice and stir to combine.

4. Divide the crackle mixture evenly between 12 regular muffin liners or use mini patty pans to spread the mixture further. Place muffin liners in a muffin pan to make the filling process easier.

5. Place chocolate crackles in the fridge to set. Remove from fridge just prior to serving. As coconut oil melts above 25°C/78°F, these treats are best stored in the refrigerator until serving time.

Chocolate crackles are a children's party staple loved by many but the classic recipe includes icing sugar, rice cereal and Copha. The Copha is especially concerning as it is a hydrogenated oil. Hydrogenation occurs when a vegetable oil is heated to high temperatures and unsaturated fats are chained to saturated fats. This results in a more stable oil that is less prone to spoiling but turns fatty acids into trans fats, something you definitely don't want your children ingesting!

CHERRY SURPRISE CHOCOLATE CUPS

Taking inspiration from the much loved Peanut Butter Cup, this raw chocolate contains a sweet surprise once you bite into it. The great thing about this recipe is that it's quick and easy to make, and the filling is entirely up to you. Try filling with a nut butter, whole chunks of fruit, homemade low sugar jelly ... the only limit is your imagination!

(MAKES 6 LARGE OR 12 MINI CHOCOLATE CUPS)

Chocolate cups

1/2 cup coconut oil, melted

1/2 cup raw cacao

1 tbsp rice malt syrup

Pinch of sea salt

Filling

1/2 cup pitted cherries
(approx 10 cherries)

1/3 cup macadamia nuts

1/3 cup shredded coconut

1. Prepare the raw chocolate by whisking coconut oil, raw cacao, rice malt syrup and salt in a bowl.

2. Prepare the filling by blitzing cherries, macadamias and shredded coconut in a food processor or using a hand blender.

3. On a small plate or tray, lay out the patty pans for filling.

4. Use a tablespoon or small scoop to pour the base layer of chocolate into each patty pan. Place tray in the refrigerator for 5 – 10 minutes to harden.

5. Remove tray from refrigerator and use a teaspoon to scoop the cherry mixture into each patty pan. Aim to keep the filling in the middle of each chocolate cup.

6. Evenly pour remaining raw chocolate mixture into each patty pan, covering the filling. Return to the refrigerator for 5 – 10 minutes to set the top layer. Store in the refrigerator ... if they last that long.

CHICKPEA CHOCOLATE
CHIP COOKIES

The sweetness in this recipe comes from the dark chocolate, use only the best quality and the darker the better (use minimum 70% dark chocolate). If you'd rather omit the chocolate, you can add chopped walnuts or cacao nibs for something different. If using either of these you may want to add a small amount of sweetener to the dough such as stevia or dextrose.

1 can of chickpeas (400g)

²/₃ cup plain flour

1 tsp baking powder

¹/₃ cup coconut oil, melted

2 tbsp milk (nut milk can be substituted)

1 tsp vanilla powder

1 tsp cinnamon

1 tsp nutmeg

2 tsp sea salt

115g dark chocolate

1. Preheat the oven to 175°C/347°F.

2. Rinse and drain chickpeas then add to the bowl of a food processor.

3. Puree until smooth then add in flour and baking powder.

4. Scrape down the sides of the bowl then add in coconut oil, milk, vanilla powder, cinnamon, nutmeg and sea salt. Pulse until combined.

5. Roughly chop chocolate into pieces and stir through.

6. Line an oven tray with baking paper, roll the dough into small balls and place 10cm apart. Use a fork to press each ball down.

7. Bake for 20 minutes.

Without the high sugar content and other additives you may find in a store bought cookie, these treats are best consumed within a day or two of baking and of course shared around! Store bought chocolate chip cookies can have around 37g of sugar per 100g so don't expect these cookies to taste nearly as sweet.

PEANUT BUTTER CUP MUFFINS

2 cups plain flour

2 tsp baking powder

1 zucchini

½ cup raw cacao

1 tsp stevia

1 tsp salt

2 eggs

1 cup of milk

100g dark chocolate (70% minimum), roughly chopped

Peanut butter

1. Preheat the oven to 180°C/356°F.

2. Sift flour and baking powder into a large bowl.

3. Grate zucchini and add to the flour along with raw cacao, stevia and salt.

4. In a small bowl whisk eggs and milk. Add wet ingredients to the dry ingredients and stir through until just combined.

5. Add chocolate and stir through.

6. Line a muffin tray with 12 liners and spoon a small amount of the batter into each. You should just cover the base of the liner and come no further up than ⅓.

7. Spoon up to a teaspoon of peanut butter into the middle of each muffin then top with extra batter.

8. Bake in the oven for approximately 20 minutes or until an inserted skewer comes out clean.

Conclusion – Life's too short

It's a phrase thrown around a lot; life's too short to work at a job you don't love, life's too short to waste a sunny day indoors ... and life's too short not to enjoy the occasional sweet treat. There's cutting the unnecessary sugar out of everyday life and then there's cutting the sweetness out of life entirely.

Of course it's completely up to you whether you bend the "rules" or stick to them, but life really is too short not to have a piece of cake at a wedding, or try a macaron when visiting Paris, if that's what you really want to do. Don't feel bad about this decision, own it and enjoy it.

Release yourself from the pressure of being perfect; if your body isn't happy with what you're feeding it, it will let you know. But sometimes that birthday cake, Christmas pudding or even an Easter egg slides down with not one headache or feeling of remorse, and that's most likely because you really wanted it and enjoyed it.

Removing the excess sugar every day allows for those moments of indulgence where the sweetness can really be appreciated and savoured. Just remember to know your limits; once you lower your sugar intake your tolerance for sweets is dramatically altered. Keep educating yourself on your Low Sugar No Sugar journey, never tire of reading a new article or book on the subject, or from trying a new recipe.

Remember that life is sweeter with less sugar, and your health and well-being is worth a lot more than the short-lived pleasure of a chocolate bar.

RECOMMENDED READING

Fat Chance, Robert H. Lustig, Hudson Street Press, 2012

Sweet Poison, David Gillespie, Penguin Books, 2008

The Sweet Poison Quit Plan, David Gillespie, Penguin Books, 2010

Pure, White and Deadly, John Yudkin, Penguin Books, 2012 reprint

Sugar Blues, William Dufty, Grand Central Life & Style, 1975

I Quit Sugar, Sarah Wilson, Pan Macmillan Australia, 2013

Useful websites

www.lowsugarnosugar.com
Visit the official blog of *Low Sugar No Sugar* for up to date information, articles and bonus recipes.

www.howmuchsugar.com
(David Gillespie's *Sweet Posion* website. Some sections of the site are for paying members only but there's a great forum to utilise for free.)

www.iquitsugar.com
(Sarah Wilson's *I Quit Sugar Website* is a growing empire with an increasing database of experts offering their tips.)

www.sugarstacks.com
(See how your favourite foods stack up in the sugar count.)

www.simplysugarandglutenfree.com
(Great for recipe ideas, substitute with your sweetener of choice.)

www.sugarfreemom.com
(Blog with plenty of recipe ideas to try.)

Social Media

Liking a Facebook page or following someone on Twitter is a great way to keep up to date with current articles and videos about the low sugar movement. It also connects you with other likeminded people who can help you on your low sugar journey.

Low Sugar No Sugar

"Like" the official Low Sugar No Sugar Facebook page and help build the community!
www.facebook.com/lowsugarnosugarbook

Follow Low Sugar No Sugar on Twitter
https://twitter.com/lowsugarnosugar

Low Sugar No Sugar on Pinterest
http://www.pinterest.com/lowsugarnosugar/

David Gillespie's Sweet Poison
**www.facebook.com/pages/
Sweet-Poison/157501174289687**

Sugar Is Killing Us Campaign
www.facebook.com/sugariskillingus

Sarah Wilson's I Quit Sugar
www.facebook.com/iquitsugar

INDEX

Agave nectar 12

Alcohol 19

Apples 15-17

Aspartame 21, 26

Balsamic vinegar 30

Berries 15-18, 33, 58, 62, 67, 99, 101, 105, 118

Blood sugar 8, 10, 28, 37, 45, 67, 105

Breakfast 12, 17, 21, 26, 33, 41, 54-69

Cacao 45, 69, 95, 97, 102, 104, 106, 108, 119, 121, 124

Cane sugar 10, 12

Chia seeds 62-63

Children 4, 16, 25, 44, 54, 112-125

Chocolate 4, 15, 22, 24, 36, 38, 41, 44-45, 94, 102, 108, 119, 123-124

Christmas 15, 17, 126

Chromium 28-29, 37

Cinnamon 45, 60, 62-63, 67, 69, 92, 109, 121, 123

Cloves 45

Coconut oil 45, 51, 55, 58, 59, 60, 63, 64, 78, 80, 83, 91-92, 104, 106-107, 109-110, 115-116, 119, 121, 123

Cravings 25, 27-30, 34, 36-38, 45

Crystalline fructose 12

Corn syrup 10, 12

Desserts 21, 24-25, 41, 45, 94-111

Dessert wine 20

Detox 11-12, 22, 24-25, 27-29, 34, 36-37, 45

Dextrose 12, 20, 34, 94, 98, 101, 103, 118-119

Diabetes 5, 6, 9-10

Dinner 38, 82, 84

Dips 48-51

Dried fruit 17, 21, 27, 41, 54

Easter 5, 15, 24, 126

Evaporated cane juice 12

Fatty liver disease 9

Fever 36

Fructose 6, 8-12, 16-21

Fruit 8, 16-18, 21, 25, 33-34

Fruit juice 8, 17, 21, 27, 29, 75

Fruit juice concentrate 12

Fruit sugar 12

Galactose 10, 12

Glucose 8, 10, 12, 20

Headaches 28, 36

Heart disease 6, 9, 10-11

Immunity 5-6, 9, 19, 30

Irritability 36

Lactose 10, 12, 37

Levulose 12

Liver 8-10, 12, 27

Lunch 17, 26, 90

Magnesium 18, 28, 37, 45

Maltose 10, 12, 20

Malt syrup 12

Maple syrup 18-20, 61

Molasses 12

Nausea 28, 36

Obesity 4, 10

Overweight 4-5, 9

Protein 25, 27, 29, 37

Raw honey 18-19, 21, 63, 67, 69

Raw sugar 12

Recipes 47-125

Red wine 19

Rice malt syrup 20, 34, 52-53, 58, 62-64, 67, 94-95, 97, 99, 102, 104-106, 108, 116, 121

Salads 40, 70-72, 75, 78, 87-88

Sauces 4, 8, 12, 21, 24, 48-49, 52-53

Snacks 12, 40-41, 43, 70, 77, 79, 94-95, 106-109

Soft drinks 4, 8, 17, 21-22, 29, 36, 118

Stevia 20, 26, 34, 67, 94, 118-119, 124

Saccharine 21

Sorbitol 21

Soup 40, 60, 68, 70, 74, 80

Sucralose 21

Sucrose 10, 12

Tonic water 19

Turmeric 27, 45, 84

Supermarket 9, 11, 20, 30-31, 41, 42-45, 48, 54, 70, 82, 112

Watermelon 15

White wine 20, 49, 53

Yoga 28, 37

Zinc 18-19, 37